WAITING TO LIVE

DR. ASA DON BROWN, PH.D.

iUniverse, Inc.
New York Bloomington

Waiting to Live

iUniverse books may be ordered through booksellers or by contacting:

iUniverse
1663 Liberty Drive
Bloomington, IN 47403
www.iuniverse.com
1-800-Authors (1-800-288-4677)

ISBN: 978-1-4502-3672-0 (pbk)
ISBN: 978-1-4502-3675-1 (cloth)
ISBN: 978-1-4502-3673-7 (ebook)

Printed in the United States of America

iUniverse rev. date: 6/15/10

To my family,
I thank you for always believing in me,
trusting in me,
accepting me,
and unconditionally
loving me.

Love always and forevermore,

Asa

WHAT ARE YOU WAITING FOR?

Do not dwell in the past, do not dream of the future,
concentrate the mind on the present moment.

—Buddha

Individuals throughout the history of humankind have waited to live. You may have heard about the individual who was working on the job and suddenly passed away of a heart attack. You may have heard about the mother who was suddenly diagnosed with breast cancer who did not make it. You may have heard about the father who died suddenly from prostate cancer. You may even have heard about the child who died tragically from falling into a lake and drowning. Unfortunately, life is a risk, but it is up to you to live it. Life is about living, here and now, so why are you waiting to live?

THE ULTIMATE QUESTIONS

Only when we are no longer afraid do we begin to live.

—Dorothy Thompson

Before we begin, I am going to ask you to answer the following questions. As you begin your journey through this book, keep the following questions in mind.

1.) What does it mean to live?

2.) What does it mean to live life?

3.) Am I living life, and am I living life abundantly?

4.) What does it mean to live a life filled with peace?

5.) What does it mean to find peace, joy, and happiness?

6.) Is it possible to experience two emotional states simultaneously?

7.) Can I experience sadness and happiness simultaneously?

8.) What is happiness?

9.) What is sadness?

10.) Is happiness a feeling, an emotion, or a state of being?

11.) Can I experience real happiness on a continuum?

12.) Does happiness have an emotional expression?

13.) Can I experience happiness despite the circumstances surrounding my life?

14.) Does happiness end when bad things occur?

15.) What makes me feel happy?

16.) Am I a person filled with fear, stress, anxiety, or anger?

17.) How do I see myself? Am I a person that is living or waiting to live?

EXPERIENCING THE JOURNEY
OF DR. BROWN'S BOOK THROUGH REVIEWS

Life is a succession of moments. To live each one is to succeed.

—Corita Kent

Son,

Your insights from your education and lifelong experiences are certainly reflected in this book. Having spent 25 years in the corporate world working with people, I have found that happy people are productive people. This book lays out the roadmap to happiness that many people just don't get. I believe your book will not only lead people to happiness, but it will make them more productive, thus reinforcing their happiness.

To me, happiness is founded in my faith in God. This faith allows me to always have hope, as I know God wants good things for me. Most of all, my faith allows me to love and be loved.

Love,
Dad

H. Don Brown, SPHR,
GPHR Global HR Consultant,
Texas, USA

I enjoyed hearing what Asa had to say about happiness in his book. What I got from it was that happiness cannot be achieved by the way that people make us feel because that changes all the time-nor events, nor material things, nor achievements in our life. It is a balance of everything.

Love,
Mama

Leah M. Brown,
Freelance Artist/Photographer L. B. Creations,
Texas, USA

I found the message thought-provoking and inspiring. The strength in the knowledge that my happiness comes from loving and caring for my own spirit is empowering. I am taking life-changing lessons from these powerful and well-written words.

Dr. Tracy L. Brown,
O.D., Optometrist
Cariboo Eyecare Clinic,
British Columbia, Canada

I have never known so much about love, the styles of love, or the definitions therein. I feel this is a highly intellectual and informative book. I am elated for your wisdom and strides that you have made in your life.

Eddie Allen Brown,
AAS, Occupational Therapist Assistant
Reliant Rehabilitation,
Texas, USA
U.S. Army Retired

Knowing the author personally, I can attest that the writer penned this work from profound insights that he has lived, experienced, and practiced as a clinical psychologist: that people are positively defined by how they overcome obstacles or are negatively influenced by living down to criticism and self-doubt. The work is philosophically, psychologically, and clinically sound and argues well that, by being taught how to take personal responsibility for our existence, we can recreate ourselves to reach our true potentials. We are more than our past behaviours and circumstance. Indeed, we can be more than, in spite of or because of, our individual or collective checkered past. The book delivers a good read and validates the promise that no matter what happens in our life, by learning how to forgive and taking positive action, giants will fall.

Dr. Chris Montoya, Ph.D., Psychology,
Tenured Professor
Thompson Rivers University,
British Columbia, Canada

Dr. Brown is a believer in unconditional love, that we all should practice it all the time. He shows us how it is achieved, what its characteristics are, and what its results will be. He claims that the human body is simply a cargo container, carrying our spiritual nature to our next destination. Moreover, the cargo container does not represent the merchandise within it, no more than the human body represents its spiritual cargo. While we look at the human body and contemplate its beauty, we usually fail to realize that the eternal being, the spirit within us, has the greater beauty, because its essential characteristic is its unconditional love.

Dr. Robert E. Clarke, Th.D.,
Emeritus Professor
Oklahoma Baptist University,
Texas, USA

I found this message of unconditional love to be an eye-opener. I never really thought about the depth of where it comes from; I just took it for granted. It is very interesting and inspirational to know the depth and meaning behind where this love comes from and how we can or have possibly achieved it.

Cheyanne Erickson, B.M.
Pembina Medical Clinic,
Alberta, Canada

Unconditional love is an emotion all of us desire. This reference helps us to understand a way that we can all achieve this emotion. It promises a sense of hope to all those that read it.

Melanie Ingram,
CLXT, Combined Laboratory and X-Ray Technologist
Saskatoon Health Region,
Saskatchewan, Canada

I concur that unconditional love is very important and essential for true happiness. Reading this has reaffirmed my belief that unconditional love is the primary ingredient for true happiness. Great read!

Travis Mullin, B.Sc.,
Commercial Pilot, Air Canada,
and
Brenda Mullin, B.Ed.,
Elementary School Teacher,
Notre Dame School
Alberta, Canada

Having known the author for over 30 years, I can say without any reservations that Asa Brown knows and lives what he has written in this publication. It is a good tool to have as a reminder that we as humans strive to be better people by treating those closest to us, whether it be friend, family, or coworker, not to be judgmental and to treat those closest to us with unconditional love. In the years I have known Asa, he continues to practice this which is written each and everyday, personally and professionally. We should take a page from this book and strive to treat our fellow counterparts as we ourselves would like to be treated.

Richard T. Conner
Lifelong Friend of Dr. Asa Don Brown
Hertz, Oklahoma, USA

Very mind-opening and insightful, made me think in different ways, made me want to read more of his book.

Mike Boehm,
Master Technician
Lake City Ford, British Columbia, Canada

Having the pleasure of knowing Asa for a number of years, he is always a pleasure to talk to and provides insight and inspiration in life. It is of no surprise to me that his written works would also give one pause for thought and make you want to focus on becoming a better person. In reading this wonderfully inspired work, I am looking forward to reviewing all of his written works—now and future—and recommending them to patients, family, and friends.

Dr. Sheila Boehm, D.C., Chiropractor
Cariboo Chiropractic,
British Columbia, Canada

Dr. Asa Don Brown has successfully managed to amalgamate his own profound insights with centuries-old wisdom and contemporary psychology to produce a unique, lucid, and pragmatic work. His book will undoubtedly inspire those seeking inspiration, educate those seeking an education, and edify those seeking an edification. In a world where many are often making more but feeling less, this book will be a welcome addition to aid them in reconciling this frustrating chasm.

Dr. Tony Mann, O.D., Optometrist
Londonderry Eye Care,
Alberta, Canada

Awesome read! Asa Brown addresses the issue of an unconditional love of self that is needed before you can accept or love others unconditionally. He further explains this concept in such a way that it encompasses and reaches all audiences. As a guidance counselor, I love the idea of writing yourself a love letter that accepts self unconditionally. This would be an especially effective strategy to use with students I counsel in a public school setting. This strategy would encourage them to look deeper into their internal self rather than always the superficial external self! I recommend this book wholeheartedly.

Earline Lawrence, M.Ed., Counselor
Garfield County High School,
Montana, USA

Very thought-provoking and intriguing concepts of the unconditional mind.

Dr. Mark Gracia, M.D.,
Emergency Room Physician
Cariboo Memorial Hospital,
British Columbia, Canada

Unconditional love from an evolutionary point of view is a short story to extinction. Without the two lesser loves, physical and brotherly, there is no foundation for the third. Right, wrong, or otherwise, most people in society probably don't think this deep and would squander the love given to them.

Ian Klepsch,
Professional Realtor
Remax,
British Columbia, Canada

The title of this book is intriguing. It led me to want to open the book, see the table of contents, skim through the first chapter for main ideas and to see where the reading might lead. As I did that, I felt myself immediately engaged, both intellectually and spiritually. By the time I journeyed through the first chapter, I found myself entering into mental dialogue with the author, feeling spiritually and intellectually challenged, and wanting to learn more. For those of us interested in and seeking spiritual wisdom, this book is one that is a must-read! It is so well written and one that will serve well for individuals across all walks of life, as well as a resource for professionals. The material herein is a work that obviously reflects the author's personal spiritual journey and wellness as well as professional excellence, driven also by a sincere caring for fellow humans, an uncommon combination in the area of self-help books.

Dr. Brown eloquently describes the intended and inherent beauty of the spirit's unconditional love. By nature, humans have—as he denotes—a trusting, open, faith-based spirit. It is indeed through contamination by contrary experiences such as negative information, situations, and events that the human spirit learns to not trust, to close off, or build walls in conscious and unconscious efforts to protect the self, an unhealthy skepticism, a change in perception of things interpersonal, a hardening of the heart (spirit) and, as Dr. Brown notes, conditional parameters pertaining to love. Yes, one only has to look at the facial expressions and behaviors of an infant and then contemplate the same reflections in later human development to know the truth of this!

As a registered psychologist, I am often guiding individuals in the area of cognitive, emotional, and behavioral matters and working on strategies with them. As Dr. Brown indicates, our thoughts are so important to our daily reality and outcomes in life. Years ago, Dr. Norman Vincent Peale also put forward some similar concepts and spiritual principles in his book As a Man Thinketh. *One notes as well that across both many religions and cultures, there is evidence of mankind struggling with the issue of mind, body, and spirit over time. Dr. Brown's book is a wonderful and timely contribution that certainly sheds light on the issues and provides hope for healthy resolution and joyful, peaceful living.*

Dr. Eunice Johannson, Ph.D., R. Psych, Neuropsychologist
Insight Psychological, Inc.,
Alberta, Canada

DEDICATION

The content of this work is dedicated to those who are

seeking a life of meaning,

seeking a life of substance, and

seeking a life completely saturated in authentic happiness

CONTENTS

A man is but the product of his thoughts. What he thinks, he becomes.

—Mahatma Gandhi

CHAPTER ONE

INTRODUCTION

How much of human life is lost in waiting?

—Ralph Waldo Emerson

Our lives have become a perpetual waiting game. This is a societal norm. We spend an absurd amount of time simply waiting. Social psychologists have described our willingness to wait as an adaptive behavior that is developed throughout our lives. We learn to conform to this waiting game through the influence of our parents, teachers, and others who play important roles during our developmental process. It has been programmed into our conscious and subconscious minds that we are to believe and think that waiting is an acceptable means to an end. We have become a global community that relies on patience, because waiting has become the norm.

We spend countless hours waiting for the cab, train, plane, and other forms of transportation to arrive, only to deliver us to another destination. Then, presumably, we will play the whole waiting game again. We wait for parcels to arrive and others to be delivered. We patiently wait for payday, but dread the day that we have to pay the bills. We spend time waiting for the red light to turn green only to be delayed the privilege to move by the driver ahead chatting on a cell phone. It is acceptable to wait in grocery lines, fast-food lines, and government lines, but only to a point. We wait for the person to arrive from afar and others to return home. We wait for our computers to upload or download documents, always thinking, "Boy, wouldn't it be nice to have a faster computer?" We spend time waiting, waiting, and waiting while wondering how long we will have to wait. We are bombarded by waiting. The waiting cycle includes the tangible and the intangible. It includes our friends, our enemies, our associates, our colleagues, our classmates, and the virtual unknowns. Waiting and patience have become synonymous, or so we think.

As a society, while we have been programmed to be patient, we have also been programmed to expect items instantly. Consider the fast-food line. You would not expect a meal served by a fast-food vendor to take more than a few minutes, so if you waited 30 minutes for it, you would have a discussion with the manager. It is interesting that our society has developed patience for lines, but has placed limits on their ability to prove patient. I am willing to wait *n* number of minutes for this item, but I am not willing to spend more than *n* for this other item. Why is it that we have placed so many expectations on waiting. In fact, we reside in a society of instant gratification, but with a measure of patience. If I am not gratified, then you will know it.

Now ask yourself this: Have you ever considered your life to be a part of the waiting game? Have you ever counted the number of days you have left until you leave for a vacation? Are you counting down the days you have left working for your employer? Have you counted the days left until retirement? Do you know the day and the time that you will graduate from school? Have you fabricated an idea of what life will be like when you leave school, stop working, or leave for that vacation?

Sadly, a majority of individuals spend their lives in a holding pattern, not unlike a plane that is waiting on the tarmac. They are in a holding pattern, waiting for the signal that may allow them to take flight. We have become so accustomed to the waiting pattern that we cannot perceive a life without waiting. We gasp with aggravation and proclaim that we are annoyed by the waiting game, yet we seek it out. While knowing that the causation of our annoyance is derived from the waiting game, ironically, we place the same pattern on our own lives.

Let me clarify that this book's intent is not to challenge the physical waiting game associated with public lines; rather, it is to challenge the personal belief system behind why we wait to live. Therefore, I ask you this most prudent question: Are you waiting to live life?

CHAPTER CHALLENGE: **THE WAITING GAME**

1.) Have you ever found yourself waiting in line at a supermarket or retail store? Were you capable of proving patient?

2.) Have you ever been forced to wait for someone else? How did you react?

3.) Have you ever felt burdened by someone else's tardiness? How did you respond?

4.) Have you ever made someone else late for an appointment? How did they react? How did you feel?

5.) Would you describe yourself as patient or as an intolerant waiter?

6.) Are you waiting to really live life until you can afford it?

7.) Does life seem impossible to live?

8.) Do you get impatient waiting for others?

9.) What situations trigger your impatience? Dealing with children? Colleagues? Family? Friends?

10.) Are you avoiding living life?

11.) Are you scared of living life?

12.) Are you uncertain what it means to live life?

If you are interested in living life and living it abundantly, then the following will interest you. Living life is accepting the realization that life must be lived and experienced on a daily basis. Living life is an exercise of the mind, body, and spirit. You can train yourself to live life consciously and subconsciously. The training of your mind can be achieved through a variety of physical, cognitive, and spiritual exercises such as daily meditation, relaxation, journaling, praying, exercising, listening to and reading positive literature, and communication with others who offer a positive mindset. Living life does not have to be delayed, but can begin today, and can begin within you.

Relax and Meditate Daily	Journal Your Inner Thoughts	Practice Focused Breathing

CHAPTER TWO

CHANGING THE PATHWAY OF OUR THOUGHTS

> As a single footstep will not make a path on the earth, so
> a single thought will not make a pathway in the mind. To
> make a deep physical path, we walk again and again. To
> make a deep mental path, we must think over and over the
> kind of thoughts we wish to dominate our lives.
>
> —Henry David Thoreau

Critical or negative thinking is a way of life, or is it? We are programmed from our inception to think on the negative. We are taught to be realistic. We are taught not to fantasize or indulge in childlike daydreams or behaviors. The very nature of our physical being is influenced by the negative perspective of life. Even in childhood, we hear riddles and rhymes that have negative connotations:

Step on the crack and you'll break your mother's back.

Step on a nail and you'll put your father in jail.

Step in a hole and you'll break your mother's sugar bowl.

Step on a line and you'll break your mother's spine.

Step in a ditch and your mother's nose will itch.

Critical or negative thinking and communication have become a way of life. In fact, our modern media moguls have recognized this and pounce on the opportunity to report negative news like a fierce bird swooping down for its prey. Today's broadcasters use television and radio shows, newspapers, magazine articles, compact discs, and books to exploit messages of negativity. Negativity sells.

If you watch a news channel for one day, you will hear stories of mayhem and pandemonium, but rarely will you hear a story of human compassion and empathy. News channels and other media outlets can't be held solely responsible for this, because we as a society have helped foster these negative voices and headlines. You hear the story of a senator caught having an affair, but it is seldom that the story ends with the news report. Instead, you hear the story being gossiped at company water coolers, coffeemakers, and lunch breaks. You may gossip of the affair in your own personal social circles, thinking not of the decay that it is causing those around you. These messages of negativity are systemic; they are capable of influencing each person within our circle of life and beyond. Think of the messages as being plaque in the human arteries, or atherosclerosis, a build-up of fat and cholesterol deposits in the human arteries. Similar to a clogged artery, if we communicate negativity, we block the pathways of positivity. Therefore, in time, these negative messages cannot only block positive communications but also cause the human spirit to decay, ultimately carrying with them a death sentence.

Death? How can negative messages carry with them the sentence of death? Let me ask you to ponder for a minute: Have you met someone who has a void in their life? Have you ever met someone who speaks of giving up? If so, you have probably met someone who has been infected by negativity. Have you ever been affected by negativity?

Several years ago, the television show "Saturday Night Live" had a skit called "Debbie Downer." The intent of this skit was to show how one person, Debbie, could have an influence on the lives of others. The skit always portrayed Debbie as being a cynical individual who was doubtful, contemptuous, and suspicious of the intentions of others. It was of little to no concern of Debbie's how her pessimistic views might have an impact on events or circumstances going on around her. She was self-centered and self-loathing.

If you consider Debbie as being the catalyst of all negativity, then you might realize that negativity itself only precipitates negative thinking and communication. Why, then, would you choose to speak or think negatively? Why would you allow others to speak or communicate negative messages in your presence? What do you gain from speaking or hearing negative communication? We cannot avoid all negative communication; rather, it is what we choose to do with the negative communication once received. Negative messages act as a prompt for change. We can either influence others to make positive choices or negative choices by the messages that we communicate and how we communicate them.

Who has been your Debbie Downer? Have you ever known a Debbie Downer? How do you react around a Debbie Downer? What are your desires when you see a Debbie Downer enter the room? Have you ever been the Debbie Downer in your circle of friends?

CHAPTER CHALLENGE: EMOTIONAL RATING SCALE

Try this task when you are struggling with negative thoughts. Sometimes, it is good idea to consider assessing and providing a rating to those thoughts. In the following chart, you will identify whether or not an event in your life was positive or negative. You will express the type of feelings and emotions associated with the event, using words such as *sadness, nervousness, anger, rage, love, adoration, worthiness*, and so forth. It is important to place a level on your overall thoughts such as *intense, strong, moderate*, or *mild*. You should indicate whether you have identified with the event by *yes* or *no*. Finally, you should consider assigning a percentage to this experience, using 0% as the worst and 100% as the best, that describes the overall effect of the event on you.

The following chart includes a few examples of how to rate your thoughts:

Negative or positive event	Emotions/ feelings involved	Level of emotion or feeling	Identify with the event?	Percentage assigned
Negative	Sadness	Moderate	Yes	30%
Positive	Excitement	Strong	No	70%

Relax and Meditate Daily	Journal Your Inner Thoughts	Practice Focused Breathing

CHAPTER THREE

CHANGING THE WAY WE THINK AND COMMUNICATE

> It is not the strongest of the species that survive, nor the
> most intelligent, but the one most responsive to change.
>
> —Charles Darwin

Change occurs and it endures. Are you adaptable to change? Are you amenable to change? What halts your ability to accept change? How do you see yourself? Do see yourself as flawless or having areas that could use improvement? An open and responsive person is an individual who is accepting of growth, adaptation, and persuasion. If I am willing to change, then I am willing to accept myself in spite of my failures or my successes. Why change? What does it mean to change?

During the 2008 U.S. presidential campaign of Barrack Obama, he proclaimed a need for change. In fact, his campaign slogan was, *Change you can believe in.* It took flight like a kite in a gusty storm. Barrack Obama's tailwind had an effect both on the American spirit as well as the global community at large. He drew in unprecedented number of minorities and had a large majority following. My intent is to use this modern-day example of how the concept of change has been used to facilitate hope, transformation, and resiliency. The public saw change as something needed for the direction of the culture at that time. Mr. Obama's camp would eventually win the Office of the President.

Let's return to the concept of change. What is it? Change is to transform an idea, an image, or a physical object from one state of being to another. Change is helping something or someone to become different. The amount of change differs depending on the intent of the manipulator. Manipulating change in self or someone else can prove a grueling experience. If change is forced, then the process of change will take time and may take a toll on your being.

When we think of the word *metamorphosis*, we commonly associate it with the life cycle of a butterfly. I am going to take you on the journey of a different creature: The salmon and its transformation or metamorphic

9

process. Salmon undergo a radical transformation of their physical bodies when leaving their saltwater habitats to enter freshwater environments. In fact, the physical changes within the composition of the salmon are drastic, indeed. The salmon undergoes a nearly complete physical metamorphosis. The salmon experiences changes within the composition of its hormones, fatty composition, enzymes, skin pigmentation, and blood chemistry. It is also known that during the migration of the salmon from saltwater to freshwater that the salmon will begin to show some sexual dimorphic characteristics such as large humps and hooked jaws. Additionally, the salmon's arteries become clogged, muscles weaken, and their skin thickens all during the process of migration. Interestingly enough, the salmon's body goes through such profound changes that at the end of its journey to spawn, it is in such a weakened state that it dies from physical exhaustion. What if you knew your journey's end? What if you had knowledge of the day your life would end? Would you approach this life differently? What would you change? If we really desire change, then we, too, can experience a metamorphosis within our being.

Change: How much do you want it? Change: How much do you need it?

CHAPTER CHALLENGE: CHANGING OUR THOUGHTS

Have you ever heard of negative or positive self-talk? Self-talk is the formulation of thoughts put into words consciously and unconsciously. Self-talk reflects your innermost feelings. Through self-talk, you can express approval or disapproval of yourself. Changes in your self-talk can improve the entirety of your being, including your mind, body, and spirit. When our self-talk is negative, we enrich our deepest fears, anxiety, and phobias. If you don't believe in your positive self-talk, the past negative self-talk will be at the forefront of your mind. Changing our being begins through changes we make in our inner-personal conversations.

Changing your inner-personal conversations:

1.) Be aware of your *I-statements*.

2.) Do not own negative self-talk. You are not your successes or failures. You are more than your mistakes, challenges, and errors. You are spirit, and it is through your spirit that you can live life fully.

3.) Focus your I-statements on the current moment, in the present tense. Do not base your I-statements on your successes or perceived failures. Be in the moment, in the present, in the now.

4.) Examples of I-statements:

        a.) I am capable of...
        b.) I am learning to...
        c.) I am willing to...
        d.) I am worthy of...
        e.) I am trusting of...
        f.) I am deserving of unconditional love, peace, joy, and happiness.
        g.) I am grateful for my life.
        h.) I am a respecter of my person.

5.) Design your own I-statements.

6.) Believe in your positive I-statements; otherwise, the I-statements will be without merit.

I-statements:

Consider writing some of your positive and negative I-statements. You may desire to review and rewrite these in a few weeks, a few months, and a year. For every negative, add a positive. It is all right to have more positives than negatives.

Be certain that your I-statements are a genuine reflection of how you feel. Be honest with yourself and your analysis of your situation. Once completed with this exercise, focus your attention daily on the positive I-statements.

Negative I-statements	Positive I-statements

Relax and Meditate Daily	Journal Your Inner Thoughts	Practice Focused Breathing

CHAPTER FOUR

PURSUING HAPPINESS

Happiness is spiritual, born of truth and love.

—Mary Baker Eddy

What is happiness? The meaning of happiness has been conceptualized, theorized, and philosophized until we have lost the basic essence of happiness. Philosophers, religious leaders, professors, psychologists, physicians, inspirational and motivational speakers, and others have all given their two cents on the meaning of happiness. In my life, I have had the fortune of working with and learning from a variety of people. In fact, I have had the privilege of learning from those individuals in society that we often overlook as well as from those we revere. Through my own life's work, I have learned that the real meaning of happiness is not some great mystery unattainable to the masses; rather, it is simplistic in its nature. The meaning of happiness is not something that we need to spend hours pondering. Haven't you ever been curious why an individual might ponder the concept of happiness? Is it that they themselves are uncertain of the meaning of happiness? Religion has told its parishioners that if you do this, then you will gain happiness. If you don't do this, then you might be eternally unhappy.

Happiness is peace. Do I have the sort of peace that passeth all understanding? What happens in my life when troubles arise? How do I respond to chaos and uncertainty? Can I be strong in the presence of disaster? If I achieve success, will I know how to handle it and be at peace with it?

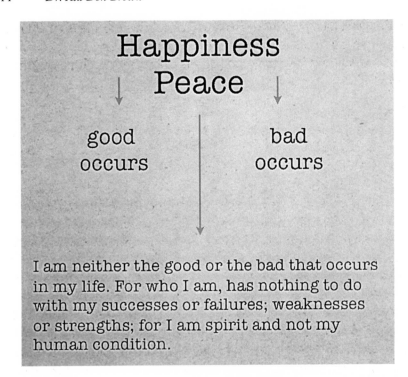

I am neither the good or the bad that occurs in my life. For who I am, has nothing to do with my successes or failures; weaknesses or strengths; for I am spirit and not my human condition.

Happiness is often mistaken for momentary delight, achievement, accomplishment, attainment, fulfillment, excitement, or success. For many, they experience what they call happiness when they receive a new job, enter a new relationship, purchase new clothes, are granted the gift of a child, and many other new experiences, but if these items represent real and genuine happiness, the flame of happiness would never cease as long as those items remained in their lives. Therefore, why are people unhappy? Why does happiness seem so unattainable? If the things that I were to achieve, receive, or accomplish in my life were the root of happiness, then I would never experience unhappiness again.

Happiness is not derived from the diplomas I achieve, the recognitions I receive, or the gratitude bestowed on me for doing something well. It is not derived from accomplishing a task or avoiding an obstacle. It cannot come from good or bad acts; otherwise, I would have to constantly achieve them. Remember that happiness and peace are not achieved through the merits of life. If I am at peace in my life, and genuinely and unconditionally love myself, then I seek to foster positivity and be a beacon of hope and life. If I am not at peace in my life and I do not have love for myself, I seek out peace and love through the lives of others. Here is the danger: If I need another to fulfill me, then I will always have to seek out that other person. If I need another to complete me, love me, respect me, accept me, or reassure me, then I will always have to go to that other person for fulfillment of these needs.

Consider the following: If I have a child and I live a life seeking out particular qualities in and/or from others, then my own child will inherently seek out qualities for their own fulfillment. The danger here is that if my child enters an intimate relationship that is unloving and without compassion, lacking in affection and acceptance, or filled with abuse and maltreatment, the likelihood that my child will leave or forsake such a relationship is slim to none. As a therapist, I have witnessed countless relationships that are egregiously constructed. I have witnessed patients display shame and embarrassment of separation because they feel such a measure would reflect on their person. I have heard many accounts of how abuse from a loved one is decaying a person's spirit, but patients feel a need to stay because the loved one is "so good to me," "believes in me," or "accepts me for who I am." All along, the abuser takes stock in knowing that they have their victim in a stranglehold, suffocating the person until they ultimately take their last breath. Sadly, I have watched many young people enter relationships filled with abuse and heartache, knowing that it is due to their lack of self-esteem, self-worth, and personal unconditional acceptance and love. If young people are taught to unconditionally love and accept themselves then find themselves in a relationship filled with hate, violence, abuse, or any other form of maltreatment, they will discard the relationship like an old pair of shoes so tattered that they can no longer be worn.

As an individual, a spirit, I need to recognize that I don't need the praise or acceptance of another. My worth and goodness are not measured by my accomplishments or failures. I am neither the good nor the bad that I do in my life. I am not what others perceive me to be or expect me to be, or a role that has been created for me to play. My life is not a reflection of my parents, my children, my spouse, or anyone else that may enter my life. I am who I am, not based on any good or bad performance of my life. If I see myself or another sees me as my failures, then I will never shed this image and will always feel down about my failures.

For several years, following the creation of the television medium, television stars experienced the phenomenon of typecasting. The star would be labeled by the role that they portrayed on television. For many stars, their lives would never be the same. Ironically, the role that casts success on their doorstep also became the role that plagued them throughout their lives. Typecasting doesn't only involve television; it can affect the lives of actors in various media from film and stage to a variety of the performing arts. It can also affect musicians, authors, and so many others that walk the planks of this earth. Have you ever considered how it affects you and me? Yes, typecasting can intrude into the lives of those in any walk of life. Have you considered the roles that others play in your life—your mother or father, brother or sister, religious leader or teacher, boss or employee? Have you not developed a particular image or set of expectations of who they are? Have you not created an ideal role for them to play? What if they decide one day to change their role? What will be your response? What are the consequences of that role being changed? Are you going to accept them as the same person? What if the role changes for the worse? How will you treat them? Will you acknowledge them? What if the role changes for the better? How will you respond? Will you know how to respond?

Have you ever known someone who is always a perceivable failure? Have they continuously been involved with the law or some sort of dispute? Does it seem that they are always having personal difficulties or hardships? What is your image of that person? How would you respond if that person changed their habitual acts or lifestyle? It is comical to think that we would be dismayed by the improvement of another. Yet, for so many, improvement of another is a representation of one's own failure. Are we the successes or failures of others? Remember the following: Your life, the essence of your being, is not based on your own successes or failures, nor is it based on the successes or failures of anyone involved directly or indirectly in your life.

CHAPTER CHALLENGE: **PURSUING HAPPINESS**

Life is a combination of our positive and negative choices. We will find ourselves sometimes pursuing negativity while at other times pursuing positivity. Our historical life, which is not a representation of our identity, is filled with successes and failures, but—for many—the perception of their failures seem to outweigh their successes. Let's make a list of good things you have accomplished in your life—your successes. Now, let's make a list of the bad things that have occurred in your life—your perceived failures. Are they equal? Can you see yourself as the good you have done? Do you see yourself as the failures that have occurred in your life? Although you are neither your successes nor your failures, your life is filled with both. If you choose to see yourself as your failures, then you must include your successes, too. The same holds true for your successes; if you choose to see yourself as your successes, then you must also include your failures. After all, who you are—your identity, your spirit—has nothing to do with your successes or failures. You are a person designed by spirit, and you are a spirit.

The following chart includes an example of success and failure:

My successes	My perceived failures
I finished school	I failed an assignment

Why have I given this assignment if you are neither your successes nor your failures? It is to help you see that if you rely on either, then you will be stuck in the moment of those accomplishments, whether negative or positive. Our accomplishments should be historical markers rather than definitions of our person, our identity, or our spirit.

Relax and Meditate Daily	Journal Your Inner Thoughts	Practice Focused Breathing

SPENDING TIME THINKING ABOUT THE POSITIVE

When was the last time that you actively thought about the positive? Have you ever intentionally made yourself think about the positive? If not, this exercise has been designed to encourage daily positive thinking. When we think about the positive, it is contagious, affecting not only our own mental health, but the mental health of those around us.

The exercise: Fill in the appropriate answer for the following questions, then take time to think about the answers related to the questions asked. Remember to fill in the appropriate information:

1.) What in my life am I thankful for?

2.) When I am around _____(person), they make me feel worthy.

3.) I am truly blessed by _____(person) being a part of my life.

4.) In my life, _____(person) always accepted me.

5.) I felt blessed when _____(person) remembered my birthday.

6.) I have no doubt that _____(person) is a true friend.

7.) I always feel accepted by _____(person).

8.) I feel complete when I...

9.) I am good at...

10.) I feel competent at...

11.) I feel satisfaction from...

12.) I am grateful for...

13.) I am inspired by...

14.) I have always felt blessed having the following people in my life:

15.) _____ (person) always encouraged me to think good about myself.

16.) When I am around _____ (person), I feel accepted.

17.) My strengths are:

18.) My best qualities are:

Relax and Meditate Daily	Journal Your Inner Thoughts	Practice Focused Breathing

CHAPTER FIVE

OBTAINING PEACE

Peace comes from within. Do not seek it without.

—Buddha

If I am peaceful, then I am happy. You might be asking yourself, then, "How does one obtain an unwavering sense of peace?" Peace is gained through knowing oneself and having an unequivocal acceptance of oneself. It is through the unconditional approval of oneself, through the unconditional acceptance of oneself, and through the unconditional attraction and unconditional love of oneself that an individual can obtain internal peace. Peace is the knowledge that no matter what happens in my life, good or bad, that I will *be*. Peace is knowing that I am worthy, that I am intelligent, that I am likable, that I am capable, and that I *am*.

If you have conditions on your life, you cannot achieve the fullness and richness that happiness has to offer. Happiness goes beyond reason and comprehension. It allows for the human mind to forgive without question or reservation. It allows a father and mother to love their child despite the child's behaviors or attitudes, mistakes, or mishaps; it is unconditional. However, if a father or mother or any other individuals place conditions on their own love for themselves, then they will ultimately place a condition on the lives of those that they proclaim to love the most. We cannot unconditionally love another if we have not shown the same sort of unconditional love to ourselves. Love must begin inwardly; then and only then can we project it outwardly. Love is peace—peace of mind, body, and spirit.

Peace equals love. If you love yourself, then you have peace dwelling inside you. It should not matter whether life's hardships abound or its trials plague us. Nor should our presence be altered by life's successes or rewards. We should be grateful whether the fruit of life is flourishing abundantly in our lives or we have been dealt life's challenges. We should continuously strive to learn from the good and the bad—our successes and our failures. If you are truly in harmony with your own person, then you will have peace in good times and bad. In fact, peace should be the prominent trademark of your life. It should flourish despite your accomplishments or your failures. Peace should indwell the very essence of who you are as a being. It should inspire your life and motivate you to become a continuously evolving person.

I have frequently thought to myself, "If I can teach my daughter one thing, it will be the love of self unconditionally." Unconditional love and peace are obtainable, but they are only obtainable if I can learn to move beyond the conditions that I placed on my life. When conditions are placed on my life and on the lives of others, they ensure that I will never experience the depths of love and happiness.

As a therapist, I have heard all sorts of conditions. Here are a few examples of what I have heard spouses say to one another:

> "If you loved me, you would..."
> "I can't love you because you..."
> "I stopped loving them because of..."
> "I cannot love someone who abuses their body."
> "I don't think they love me, because I gained weight."
> "I can no longer go on, because they stopped loving me."
> "I no longer feel love for that person, because their physical body has changed."
> "I no longer feel accepted by that person."
> "I feel unworthy and unacceptable."

What are some of the conditions that you have placed on your life? What are some of the conditions that you have placed on the lives of others? Why? What good do the conditions serve? We place conditions on our own personal life and the lives of others to prevent harm. We have fabricated this notion that if I have conditions on my life and I place conditions on the lives of others, then I will be safe and, ultimately, I will avoid harm.

This is a slippery slope, for if I allow another to define my acceptability and my worth, then I will always have to rely on that other person. I have to stop seeing myself according to how others see me. I am neither my mistakes, my failures, my successes, nor my triumphs. My value does not increase or decrease depending on who is in my life.

If I really and sincerely desire to obtain peace, then I must move beyond the expectations and conditions that I hold for myself and those that have been placed on me.

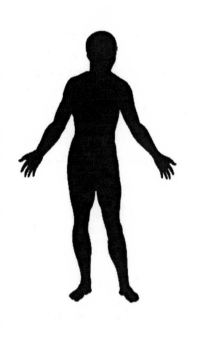
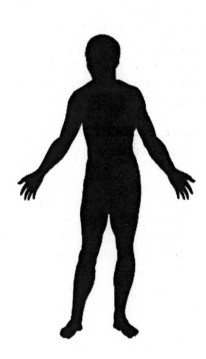

CHAPTER CHALLENGE: **BEING STILL**

Please read through this exercise before proceeding, or have a friend calmly read the instructions of this exercise to you. Begin by sitting upright in your favorite chair or on your favorite couch. Be certain that all outside distractions, noises, and sounds are silenced during this particular exercise.

Let me help you to relax and achieve harmony within your mind, body, and spirit. As you begin this process, focus your mind, body, and spirit on achieving perfect harmony, mindfulness, and ultimate calmness.

You'll need to take your shoes off for this exercise. Place your feet flat on the ground. Next, you can place a pillow on your lap, then gently place your hands folded on your lap. Do not clamp your hands together; rather, your hands should be in a relaxed state. At this point, you should have your feet flat on the floor while gently folding your hands. Next, you will begin to slowly close your eyelids. Be certain that you are not forcing your eyelids closed; rather, close your eyes as though you were preparing for a nap.

At this point, you should take a moment to breathe. Continue to keep your feet flat on the floor, your hands gently folded, and your eyelids closed. As you begin to breathe, you should begin counting to 5 in your mind—inhaling to the count of 5, exhaling to the count of 5. Continue counting to 5 as you inhale and exhale. Repeat this throughout the remainder of this exercise.

Next, you should focus your mind on the peace oriented with this moment. Focus your mind on the moment, excluding all external factors. Focus your mind on the task at hand. Breathe in and out. Breathe in and out. Continue with the task of focusing and relaxing your mind, body, and spirit. You may experience your mind trying to wander; keep your focus on the task of relaxing, breathing, and—slowly and methodically—counting to 5. If you have a metronome, focus on the metronome's repetitive sound. Be certain to set it at 120 beats per minute. If someone is reading this exercise to you, they can act as your personal metronome, repetitively counting to 5 in a calm, quiet, and methodical voice. You do not need to count if you are listening to your friend's voice. If you have a metronome, it may help you to relax if you are listening and counting to it.

At this point, you should have begun to experience a calmer and gentler state of relaxation. Now, I would like for you to focus on an imaginary sun. I want you to follow the sun from its rise to its descent. Be certain to continue counting throughout this exercise. Watch the sun and count the sun across the horizon.

You should be experiencing a state of tranquility, harmony, and full relaxation. Allow yourself to become fully and completely transfixed by your state of relaxation and peace. As you wrap up your time of meditation and relaxation, you may want to gently open your eyes, becoming aware of your surroundings. Next, you may want to reflect on this time of relaxation, allowing your mind to continue soaking up the peaceful rays of this experience. Finally, you may desire to take a moment and write about this experience. Be certain to take your time getting up and thriving in the moment at hand.

It is important to understand that each stillness experience may be different. Don't worry or fret about this. Like other events in life, your experience should and will change with each encounter. If you have found this challenging, consider retrying this exercise in a week. You may want to write about each experience you have with this form of meditation.

Please understand that you can make adaptations to this exercise. For instance, you may desire to play soft sounds like those of ocean waves or calm rain throughout your meditative process. Be certain that the sounds are not too loud or assertive. You may also desire to place candles around you, but note that too many candles may prove overbearing. Finally, it may be helpful to record yourself or someone else reading this message allowed, then listening to the message at will.

May this message prove to be a resource for calm, peace, and internal harmony.

Relax and Meditate Daily	Journal Your Inner Thoughts	Practice Focused Breathing

CHAPTER SIX

A CONDITIONAL STATE

Happiness doesn't depend on any external conditions;
it is governed by our mental attitude.

—Dale Carnegie

If you place conditions on yourself, then you place conditions on all others. Conditions are the state of consciously and subconsciously declaring that I am acceptable and worthy as long as I perform or abide to a certain standard of life.

Have you ever experienced snow? Have you ever experienced the glistening of the snow and the sun's rays shimmering on the ice? Have you ever experienced the coolness of the breeze that gently glides by you when you open your door? If so, then you can also understand the vice of the snow and the ice. Ice is temperamental and can prove very moody. It can be your friend one minute and your enemy the next. Ice holds no allegiances or loyalties. It is known for its beauty when a skater is performing his or her craft in the Olympics as well as for causing folks to fall, causing all sorts of pains and injuries. Ice is not always nice, so this is why I use it as my example today. If you were walking outside and you had a sudden fall, what would you do? What would be your immediate reaction? Have you ever fallen on ice? How did you react to the situation? Did you react? Let's consider that you are preparing for the most important engagement of your life. It is a day to celebrate like no other. You have spent countless hours preparing yourself. You are wearing the right clothes and your hair looks fabulous. You arrive at your destination. You cautiously step out of your vehicle, because you know that it is slick outside today, and you begin to walk. Suddenly, in front of a crowd of people, you slip and fall. What is your immediate reaction? Do you instinctively look around to see who has witnessed your mishap? How are you going to respond to this situation? Are you worried how others are going to perceive you? What negative words or images have you conjured up in your mind? Have you sought out blame? Are you feeling shameful about this situation?

Let's take this example one step further: What if the outfit that you are wearing was torn or blemished? What if you have dropped whatever items that you were carrying and they are now covered in dirt and grime? What happens to you emotionally if the person that you admire the most was standing nearby when this event occurred? What if you have always sought acceptance and approval from this person, but you feel as though he or she has never fully granted either? Are you going to get upset and consider yourself a failure? Will you feel as though you have been a bitter disappointment? Why? What good does it do to belittle yourself? Why discount yourself or be disgruntled with yourself over a human error? Was not this incident a mistake? Could you have prevented it, and—if you could have—does it even matter?

How can you love another if you cannot show the same unconditional love and gratitude to yourself? Conditions say, "I will accept you and love you as long as you follow these rules or guidelines." Conditions have no place in the spirit. If I place conditions on my love, then I am not fully loving myself or another. It is important to remember that if I place conditions on my own love for self, then I will have a moment in time that I can no longer love myself. I may not like everything that I am bound to do, say, or think, but I should not ever stop loving myself.

Let's discuss loving versus liking. Liking is the emotional state in which we show an acceptance, a desire, a fondness, and a personal agreeability and enjoyment of another. To like someone is to show a fondness or a selfless regard for another being. Therefore, our fondness grows into an existential experience of admiration, pleasure, and satisfaction being in the company of that other person. I don't have to like someone in order to love them. Love is a sacrificial item. Love has been defined by authors, scholars, philosophers, and religious leaders. Love goes beyond all understanding, comprehension, and persuasion. I cannot be forced to love someone. It is a gift that I not only grant to myself but to others as well. Love is an intense conscious and unconscious response to a deep inner set of emotions and feelings. True love—unconditional love—knows no limits. It is a spiritual presence in a physical body. It endures all hardships. Love is an innate drive very similar to the drives of hunger and thirst. It is, so it needs to be quenched.

I don't have to like someone in order to love them. The same is true for myself. I don't have to like my deeds, actions, or choices in order to love myself. If I love myself, I see myself beyond the outer person. The outer person—the person who makes mistakes—is not the spiritual being that resides within my body. Have you ever driven a vehicle down a particular path, time and time again, only to forget to stop by a particular destination? Have you ever found yourself at a new job only to answer the phone the way you may have been trained to answer the phone at your last job? Have you ever found yourself preparing for your day only realizing later that you were not awake during your morning routine? If so, then you can relate to the following. You are created of an outer and an inner being. Your outer being is bound to make mistakes. Your inner being is similar to Jiminy Cricket; it's your conscious, it's your spirit, it's your guide. As a collective society, we have molded these two dichotomies together, but—in truth— these two beings are distinctly different. Our physical mind is a mechanical object that relies on routine and exercise. Our spiritual mind relies on unconditional states of grace, peace, love, kindness, joy, and perseverance. As humans, we struggle with these two separate pathways. Although these pathways have been defined in a variety ways, ultimately, they are our physical mind—the brain—and our spiritual mind. Our physical mind intends no harm but struggles with what is right and wrong. The physical is a programmed component that engages when it is told to. Our minds are mechanical objects that function no different from an engine. Engines are mechanical devices that convert one form of energy into another form energy. Our physical minds are also roadmaps of instruction, calculators of equations, and diplomats of information. Our physical minds are capable and adaptable to change, and it takes physical manipulation of the components to rewire the circuits of the brain. As a mechanical force, your outer being—the brain and the body—can only act, react, and maneuver through the paths that have been engineered to be maneuvered, whereas the spiritual mind is guided and directed by intangible forces.

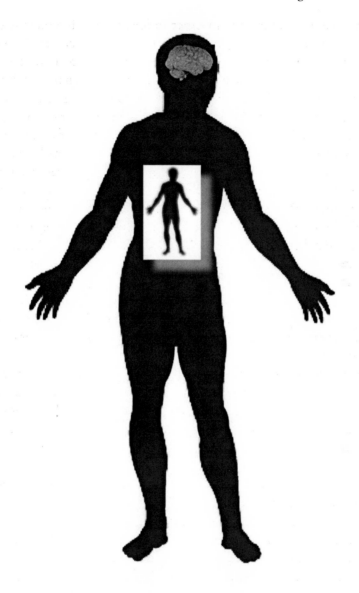

The imbalance of human presence occurs when the conditioning of our physical minds counters that of our spiritual beings. The human and spiritual conscious are not equipped for negativity. The human and spiritual conscious cannot comprehend or completely relate to negativity. Yet, it is through negative conditioning and manipulation of our physical minds that our spiritual minds become conflicted. Because our spiritual minds do not accept negativity, our physical minds become at odds with the spirit. Therefore, we become torn between what is right and what is wrong. Therefore, we become two minds struggling to gain control of the human condition.

Have you have found yourself saying, "I sincerely didn't mean to say that" to another person? Have you ever caught yourself lashing out at another person? Have you ever lost control? If so, then you are on autopilot. Our physical minds are equipped and preprogrammed to run on autopilot. If we program our minds with negativity, then negativity will certainly take over at one point or another. If we choose to program our minds with positivity, we are more apt to be prepared for any situation. If our thinking becomes negative, then we are better equipped to alter it with positivity. If our mind avoids the positive, then we are more apt to query our negativity, thus accelerating the negative to become the truth in that circumstance. If I equip my mind with negativity, I am more apt to turn to negativity in times of crisis, brokenness, and turmoil.

Let's look at the human mind in a different context. Your spirit is the driver and your physical brain is the vehicle. If the vehicle is the physical brain and the body, then it will only react as you instruct it. Moreover the physical brain—the vehicle—which is being driven by you, can only react and interact with the messages that you send it. If you turn your steering wheel to the left, then the vehicle will naturally move towards the left. If you accelerate the vehicle by placing more weight on the pedal, then the vehicle will naturally accelerate. Moreover, the physical brain is only capable of reacting and acting with the instructions that are either preprogrammed in the center of control (the engine, or the physical brain, in this scenario) or with the physical messages that you put forth. The physical brain cannot manipulate itself. The physical brain is not an engineer; it is incapable of forcing you to make choices. It has been designed to receive information and act on that information. The human brain is a complex organ that is made up of the corpus callosum, the cerebral cortex, the thalamus, the hypothalamus, the hippocampus, the brain stem, and cerebellum, and let's not forget it is the center of the nervous system; it is in essence a computer developed to interact with information programmed into its mainframe.

If the physical mind and body are altered by some sort of substance (e.g., alcohol or a chemical), they may be incapable of performing to their optimum capacity. If the human body and mind lack in nourishment and sufficient nutrients, the mind and the body will react to the lack of nutrition, causing a host of issues to be perpetuated onto the body and the brain. In fact, if the body is lacking in the proper nutrients, it can trigger a host of issues, causing difficulties with the scalp and the hair follicles; mouth diseases and disorders such as bleeding gums, tooth decay, cracked or swollen lips, discoloration and swelling of the tongue; goiter issues (thyroid); cardiovascular issues such as hypertension, atherosclerosis, poor circulation, and the possibility of heart attacks and strokes; vision issues such as night blindness, macular degeneration, retinal degeneration, and darkening around the eyes; respiratory issues such as asthma and cancer; liver failure; kidney damage; damage to the pancreas, gastrointestinal tract, urogenital tract, skeletal structure of the body, the skin, soft tissues, red blood cells, and the blood chemistry; as well as the deterioration of the neurological system. Ultimately, if you are malnourished, the body is incapable of thriving and will steal its required nutrients from its own tissues, therefore injuring and destroying itself in the process. An example of the effects of malnourishment can be seen in someone who has anorexia (a psychological and medically based eating disorder). If they live with this condition long enough, the finale of this abuse is death. Due to the extreme nature of anorexia, when coroners perform an autopsy to discover the cause of death, it is typically apparent that it was a lack of nutritional value. Nevertheless, the body is not unlike a motor vehicle. If you were to run the vehicle on very low oil, in time the engine—the operating system of that vehicle—will lose energy and seize up, thus resulting in a cease of operation of the vehicle. Our physical minds are reflective of that engine. If you stop feeding your mind or providing it the proper nutrients, it too can lose energy, seize up, and eventually cease to operate. Therefore, it is imperative that you maintain all aspects of your human condition—the mind, the body, and the spirit.

As a spirit, you have control over your physical brain. The physical brain is guided by its organic makeup, and the spirit is guided by a higher power. It is inspired to live, to think, and to be in harmony with the universe. If you follow the leadership of your spirit, it will not guide you down a path of brokeness, emptiness, and possible abandonment of who you are intended to be. Your spiritual nature wants you to live a life of harmony, peacefulness, and love.

CHAPTER CHALLENGE: ALTERING OUR THOUGHTS

When negative thoughts emerge, we have a decision to make: (a) We will either choose to walk the pathway of our negative thoughts, or (b) We will turn our backs on our negative thoughts and choose to walk a different pathway. Changing or causing change in our minds is not always an easy process. However, as your spiritual being grows, you will gain control over your physical mind. If you sincerely desire control over your negative thoughts as well as your physical mind, you must actively exercise your mind with positive literature, materials, and information. It is vitally important that you exercise your mind on a regular basis. You will find that routine exercise of your mind will empower you not only to control your own thoughts, but also to avoid damaging thoughts sent your way by others.

What if I am without materials to read and exercises to review? How can I change the pathways of my undesirable thoughts? Changing your thoughts does not always have to occur through reading materials, audiobooks, lectures, or the help of a professional. Try some of the following exercises whether you find yourself isolated from positive resources or the resources you do have seem stale at the moment.

1.) Be aware of your internal thoughts. Likewise, be aware of your mind's external influences. If you are discovering that your thoughts are going down a negative pathway, stop and recognize that the thoughts that you are thinking are merely thoughts. Your thoughts are incapable of controlling you. Your thoughts are merely thoughts of the mind. Your thoughts may be influenced by a variety of situations, persons, and history, but your thoughts do not have to become your reality. Be in charge of your mind, letting your spirit guide you.

2.) Take time to breathe when you are being challenged by your thoughts. Recognize that the thoughts you are thinking are merely thoughts and that they have no control over your being. Breathing exercises are an excellent way to clear your head, to provide focus, and to help you reengage your spiritual control.

3.) Challenge your negative thoughts by writing them down. Constructive writing goes beyond simply writing what is bothering us; it is a discourse with our own being. When transcribing your thoughts to paper, be certain that your thoughts are not seeking to place blame. Your physical mind will try to guide you down a pathway of negativity and scattered thoughts. Be in charge. Write down the thoughts you are thinking, whatever they may be, reminding yourself that this is a source of releasing negative energy, not a document to debate or side with negativity. It is a way to express those negative thoughts that are trying to take charge of your mind. Be in charge and direct your thoughts accordingly.

4.) Communication is a necessity for clearly blocked pathways. If you have negative thoughts occurring in your own mind or are approached with negativity, you should seek to clear your pathway of such destructive materials. If you are blocking another's pathway, the same applies to you, too. If you allow negative materials to reside on your pathway to health, you will be unable to move forward; therefore, your life will be stuck in place until you clear your pathway. Healthy communication is vital in recovering from a blocked pathway. If you have a blocked pathway, seek to bring clarity to the situation. Good communication clarifies our intentions, makes sense of our misunderstandings, and seeks to make peace the victor in any situation.

5.) Have you ever struggled with a negative thought? Have you ever tried to block a thought but found that the thought kept reappearing in your mind? If so, you are battling with your thoughts. You are also giving leverage to your thoughts. In some cases, your thoughts are trying to become your identity. Such thoughts may say, "I am stupid," "I am fat," I am unworthy," "I am unlovable," or "I am unbecoming." Perhaps your thoughts are seeking to dampen your spirit. When we battle our thoughts, we become defensive. We can prove positively offensive if we allow the spiritual mind to guide us. Instead of only making counter-statements such as "I am not stupid," you should declare the beauty, worth, and intelligence that reside within you. Likewise, it is important to believe what you are saying; otherwise, your mind will present other negative thoughts to block your pathway to health.

6.) Meditation is an excellent resource for altering your state of mind. It is also beneficial for the daily training of your mind, body, and spirit. The benefits of meditation are numerous:

Spiritual Benefits of Meditation

a. It can help improve your spiritual relationship, personal relationships, and inner-personal relationship.
b. It helps provide insight and can be a guide through your spiritual pathways.
c. It will improve your personal awareness of life and its direction.
d. It can unite your mind, body, and spirit
e. It will deepen your recognition and acceptance of unconditional matters.
f. It is beneficial for developing your spiritual being.
g. It can create harmony and guidance, offering an unconditional form of peace.
h. It will help you become more mindful.
i. It will deepen your recognition of the need to forgive and to love.
j. It will empower you over your mind and body.

Psychological Benefits of Meditation

a. It can improve your self-esteem, self-worth, and self-awareness.
b. It can help you become more aware of your surroundings.
c. It provides positive communication between your conscious and unconscious minds.
d. It has been shown to increase brain activity.
e. It can help eliminate your negative thoughts and empower your positive ones.
f. It helps reduce anxiety, rage, anger, frustration, and your overall stress levels.
g. It is beneficial for providing insights into your relationships.
h. It can provide clarity.
i. It has been shown to be beneficial for chronic fatigue, insomnia, and sleep-related disorders.
j. It can help with your moods, thoughts, and behaviors.

Physiological Benefits of Meditation

a. It will improve your oxygen consumption.
b. It has been shown to improve your physical energy.
c. It can help with weight loss and weight control.
d. It provides your body a time of relaxation.

e. It has been shown to enhance the immune system.
f. It will help with balance and overall body control and coordination.
g. It can help with your digestive system.
h. It can help reduce stress, anxiety, rage, anger, and frustration.
i. It can lower your stress level, allowing your body to fight off viruses.
j. It can help reduce muscle tension and restriction.

7.) Guided visualization is an incorporation of meditation and breathing. It also incorporates the concept of imagery. When using guided visualization, it is prudent to have all distractions and interferences set aside. However, in some cases, we are unable to set all worldly distractions aside, so it is sometimes a good exercise to try these techniques with distractions. Competitive snowboarders do not have the luxury of setting aside all outlying distractions. Therefore, it is important that they are capable of focusing their inner thoughts and gaining an edge competitively. How do you use guided visualization? Guided visualization is the technique of mapping out your surroundings. For a competitive snowboarder, they need to know the lay of the land, the jumps, the rails, and the various competitive obstacles that might challenge them professionally. Often, competitive athletes of all kinds do a mental play-by-play, navigating their routine from the beginning to the very end. How is this beneficial? As a professional athlete, you will have a competitive edge, because you have already run a virtual drill of the competition in your head. How can I use guided visualization? Guided visualization can be employed as a scenic getaway. If you are finding that you are stressed out, overwhelmed, frustrated, angry, and full of many other negative emotions, then it is important that you find a place in your mind that is calm. For a majority of us today, we seldom have time to enjoy the beauty of nature. Guided visualization will help you to achieve the outer beauty of life internally. You can find that place of peace and harmony. Through breathing and a meditative state, you will begin to imagine that you have entered this perfect place of peace, harmony, tranquility, and ultimate calmness. Remember that you have power over your thoughts. Guided visualization is capable of reproducing the most incredible scenes of nature, and it is also beneficial for exercising control over your conscious and subconscious minds. May you gain peace and harmony on your visual trip.

Finally, remember that you have control over you mind. What your mind tells you does not have to prove your reality. You are the master of your mind and body. Let your spirit guide you and may you flourish through these experiences.

Relax and Meditate Daily	Journal Your Inner Thoughts	Practice Focused Breathing

CHAPTER SEVEN

LOVE BEGINS THE PEACE PROCESS

The supreme happiness in life is the conviction that we are loved—loved for ourselves or, rather, loved in spite of ourselves.

—Victor Hugo

Once I begin to love myself unconditionally, then I will begin to have an unconditional love for others. I will begin to see myself through unconditional eyes. I will no longer judge myself or others by the preset conditions that I once had in my life. Remember that if I am judging another, then I am ultimately judging myself. I will accept myself, approve of myself, be confident in myself, and be secure in myself. If I reserve my love, then I will not experience the full merits of love. It is important to understand that, although I may choose to begin the process of love for myself, my human mind and the external mind may reject my desires for unconditional love based on past experiences and the operational programming that they have become accustomed to. If I have established conditions in my life and these conditions limit my ability to love myself, then I will have the same conditions for others and these conditions will limit or disable my ability to show unconditional love for others as well. It is with love that we begin the process of healing.

If I can love myself, then I can forgive myself.

If I can forgive myself, then I will choose not to judge myself.

If I reject false impressions of myself, then I will only accept my true nature.

If I can accept myself, then I will be attracted to myself.

If I am attracted to myself, then I will begin to know and be attracted to my healthy nature.

If I receive news or overhear false rumors that are trying to discredit my person, then I will have comfort in knowing what the truth is and not be swayed by these false accusations, rumors, or lies.

If I hear truths about my past and they are being used to hinder my ability to live a fruitful live, then I will have comfort in knowing that I can fully accept my past for what it is, accept that I have received forgiveness, and not allow these issues of the past to become my identity.

What is our true nature? Our true nature is the spiritual component of our lives that dwells deep within our beings. We are spiritual beings. As humans, and with the human mind, we are conditioned to place judgment on our own being as well as others. We look at our fellow humans' good attempts and bad events. Our society has taught us to see ourselves as well as other fellow humans according to our works, our deeds, and our mistakes, and not our spirits. If our fellow humans fail or make an unspeakable mistake in life, then we consider those humans according to their outer person mistakes, deeds, or actions rather than the spirit that dwells inside them.

What am I ultimately saying? We are not unsatisfactory because we make mistakes, fall short of others' or our own expectations, or commit some deplorable act in our lives. We may fall short in our physical bodies and with our physical minds. Look at any performance, whether it be of an art, sport, or any other form that comes to mind. Consider that form for a minute. We have all witnessed an event in which someone falls short of our own or their own expectations. Have we not all failed to perform at our peak in some area of our lives? Does this mean that we have brought such a disgrace to others and ourselves that we are incapable of mending and repairing the challenge that we have been faced with in our lives? Let me remind you at this very moment that we have all fallen short and that we have all failed at one moment or another in our lives. Remember this, for this is a critical point: Failure is nothing more than a challenge or a limitation that faces us head-on. Are you going to allow this challenge to limit your ability to live life to its fullest? Are you going to let your personal limitations hinder you from living life and experiencing the richness therein? Failure can account for a variety of issues. You may observe low academic scores as a failure. If you have a relationship that ends abruptly, it too may be what you consider a failure. You may consider yourself a failure if you flunk a test, lose a job, are not placed on a sports team, or forget where you placed your keys. You may see yourself as a failure if you have bad skin, a bulbous chin, or a broken leg or toe. In fact, you may even see yourself as a failure if you children fall short of a goal and/or an expectation, but the truth is that you are not a failure. Failure is only an illusion. Failure may even be viewed as the lack of success, not reaching a particular benchmark, or not obtaining a particular achievement. It may even be considered a deficit or possibly a limitation, but the truth is that failure is just a roadblock. It is an obstacle. It is not a merit of your worth or value. Failure is not your identity. You are not a failure. Even if your body fails you, your mind fails, or you fail yourself or another, these failures are simply challenges inviting you to reengage, compete, and strive for the ultimate prize of living life to its fullest.

Let me tell you a brief story about an event that took place when I was an 8-year-old child. In 1980, I had a severe medical moment in my life. My body was faced with a host of medical issues that challenged me as a person and a spirit. Before getting deathly ill, I was not unlike most children. I loved to play baseball, ride my bike, and run around town with my closest friends. My body lost its ability to thrive and live life to its fullest physically; it completely shut down. I was facing death. But, in the face of death, I recall having one of the earliest epiphanies of my life. I had a sudden revelation that began my comprehension of what it means to live life. Let me clarify at this moment that I would not always follow this path in my life, but the revelation set inside my spirit the resolve to live life to its fullest and beyond. I had a yearning that burrowed itself deep into my spirit. It was the first time I recall feeling this strange sensation of a spiritual call on my life. I want to express how we all have such calls in our lives, but we do not always choose to heed them or are alert to these callings in our lives.

During my time in the hospital, my body would be dealt a number of challenges. It felt at times as though these challenges were waiting around a corner like a child sneaking looks while playing peek-a-boo. One of my greatest medical challenges during my stay in the hospital had to do with the decay of the joints in both of my ankles. It has proven to be one of my greatest challenges of life, and this issue will still occasionally peek its head around to say *Boo!* when I am least expecting it. While I was in the hospital, the medical decision was made to replace the joints in both of my ankles. Imagine what it was like for a child all of 8 years old to be told that he may not only have difficulty learning to walk again but also that he may not ever walk again. The issue was deeper than the replacement of my joints; I had a host of medical difficulties that were challenging my body and its ability to thrive. In fact, I had severe weight loss, a weak arm due to a mishap during my stay in the hospital, and a variety of other medical concerns. The challenges facing my body were so entrenched that it was like a smorgasbord of ailments. Because I was facing all of these challenges along with the challenge of learning to walk on my new ankles, it was a truly difficult time for me. It was a time of change, a time of brokenness, a time of getting reunited with my physical person, and a time of intense learning.

Due to a lack of physical stimulus, extreme weight loss, and other medical difficulties, my body became frail and it became clear to my physicians that I may not walk again. Admittedly, it was a shock to me, but I was fortunate that my physicians saw this as an opportunity to push me to my fullest. Following my prognosis, my personal physicians sent me to physical therapy. It took weeks, months, and years to eventually overcome my physical obstacles. Although my joints have never been the same, I now have the privilege of walking, tip-toeing, and jogging. Admittedly, while in the hospital, I knew that I had to push myself, sometimes beyond what would have been considered reasonable. It was a challenge to overcome my limitation. It was a challenge to beat the odds and prove to myself and others that I could and would walk again. The experience also taught me that, although I may be challenged at times, I don't have to identify with my challenges. In fact, I may have a variety of difficulties facing me but, as I am in tune with my spirit, all outlying difficulties are mere obstacles waiting for me to go around them.

I am more the good that I do than I am the bad. If I judge myself and others based on their good merits, then I must also account for the bad merits. Therefore, although my good merits and bad merits are a part of my external persona, they are not my internal identity.

We frequently see individuals as their external identities. We have been conditioned to think that the external identity *is* the person, such as a fireman, police officer, civil servant, religious leader, teacher, lawyer, physician, electrician, or plumber. However, our true identity has little to do with the external factors of our lives. What happens to the fireman who is critically injured in a fire? What happens to those who are disabled and unable to work in their profession? Are they less of a person because they are no longer capable of working in their chosen professions? If I have viewed myself as a professor for years and I am no longer capable of teaching, then what will I do to fill the void of my profession? If I have been an author of books and my eyesight fails me, how will I see myself beyond my sight? What if I have been a criminal or have made some major errors in my life? Am I only to see myself as the negative deeds that I have enacted? If I retire from a lifelong position, will I no longer be of benefit to humanity? We seldom see ourselves beyond our professions, our deeds, and our titles. We are not our titles. I am neither the good that I do nor the bad that I commit. I am neither the accolades that have been thrust on me nor the cuffs that might bind me. My being, my presence goes beyond this physical makeup of my person. I am a spirit.

CHAPTER CHALLENGE: DEFINING LOVE

What is your definition of love?

Do you see yourself as a loving person?

Do you love yourself as you love others?

What does it mean to live an unconditional life?

Our definition of love is frequently a combination of our family's influence, our relationship encounters, and our personal insights into self. Have you equated love with peace? Do you feel that love and peace are interactive and interrelated? Defining love is different than living a life abundant with love. Love is an unconditional state of being. Love is a merciful, gentle, and passionate embodiment of the spirit that resides in us. If you unconditionally love someone, you look beyond their inadequacies, fleshly errors, and simple mistakes, and see them as a being full of life and potential. Love goes beyond the superficial, hearkening deep inside of the human spirit. Love calls for patience, kindness, peacefulness, and sincerity. Love is abundant, and it is free. Love looks beyond our faults, our failures, and our mistakes.

Genuine love, authentic love, and unconditional love are characteristics of our spirit.

Can you imagine a life without an unconditional form of love? What if all loves were represented by the commonly misspoken, misinterpreted, miscommunicated, and misguided forms of love? What am I speaking of? Have you ever heard someone declare, "Man, I love my car" or "I love my new outfit/relationship/house" or some other earthly possession? If so, then you have heard someone misuse, miscommunicate, and misinterpret the real meaning of love. Love knows no boundaries. It contains no envy or self-righteousness. Real love, genuine love, and authentic love can only be known through the leadership of spirit.

Try this as an exercise: Journal the names of those you undoubtedly love. Then look at those names and ask yourself, "Do I unconditionally love them? What if they failed me?" Then write your own name. Ask yourself if there is any form of failure that would cause you to stop loving yourself. If there is, then you have placed conditions on those particular relationships. If there isn't, then you are well on your way to living life and living it abundantly.

A LOVE LETTER

When was the last time you wrote a love letter? Were you capable of fully expressing yourself and being yourself when composing the letter? When was the last time that you received a love letter? How did it feel to receive a love letter? Did your heart pitter-patter? Did you feel butterflies in your stomach? A part of gaining insight into self-love is being capable of loving and expressing that love for others. In this exercise, you will write a tentative love letter to someone else. You may choose to write this letter to someone significant in your life, or you may choose to write an anonymous love letter. It is your choice. The love letter does not have to be delivered. It is your letter. Be certain that you have someone in mind. Write as though you had the intent to deliver the letter.

Today's date: _____

Love letter title: _____

| Relax and Meditate Daily | Journal Your Inner Thoughts | Practice Focused Breathing |

CHAPTER EIGHT

PROCESS

I have found the paradox, that if you love until it hurts,
there can be no more hurt, only more love.

—Mother Teresa

We can excuse and make excuses to uphold the condition of our thinking, but the reality is that there are no excuses for being, thinking, or acting negatively. You are responsible for your negative thoughts, actions, and reactions. Excuses are merely an attempt to blame or attach some sort of justification behind our actions, thoughts, and reactions. Excuses seek out blame while making the individual feel unnecessary shame or guilt. Excuses are not necessary and have no measure of profit.

The power of positive thinking is in my control. I am the master of my thoughts, my perceptions, and what meaning I give to my thoughts and perceptions. There are events that occur in everyone's life that will push us in the direction of negativity; they may even precipitate or encourage us to think negatively. Ultimately, though, we decide whether or not we will give into the negative thought or perception. Although we might be tempted or prompted to think negatively, we have recourse to take charge of our thoughts, because we are in charge of our thoughts. Positive thinking is empowering, even when negative thoughts or perceptions try to take control. We are capable of thinking positive in the midst of the most trying of circumstances or events. Although a negative event or circumstance might be occurring in our lives, it is how we approach the event or circumstance that makes the total difference. We might even be tempted to go down the path of least resistance, which might be negativity, but it is the acknowledgment that the thought is negative that provides our positive thoughts a platform. The platform is the place at which we can ultimately deny any negative thoughts or perceptions that try to creep into being.

If you seek to be happy, it is through the power of thought and perception that you will gain your inner stability. If you continuously think about a negative thought, you will ultimately begin to feel unhappy. The reverse is true for happy thinkers. If you change the way you see or perceive events in your life, you will ultimately begin to feel and experience genuine happiness, even in the midst of unhappy times. You can be happy—internally happy—during the most difficult of times. You might even be asking yourself, "How can I honestly and sincerely be happy despite the conditions or events occurring in my life?" Consider this: What kind of individuals do you enjoy being around? Of course, most people—if they are being honest with themselves—will say, "Happy people." On your personal journey of self-exploration, improvement, and insight, you will find that people may suddenly want to be around you. They may ask questions about what has occurred to change the very nature and demeanor of your life. They may even begin showing interest in this newly found source of happiness. Will people query the rationale behind your happiness? Most certainly. Some people will not know how to relate to your newfound source of happiness. People may even dismiss you, saying to you or others that true happiness cannot be experienced on a continuum. Again, let's reflect on the concept of happiness. Happiness is the ability to contain within yourself a true and genuine source of peace. It is a sense of peace that goes beyond all explanation and comprehension, and springs forth from your internal being, allowing you to overcome and be content with life despite whether life and the external world are proving positive or negative. This sense of peace will carry you through heartache and triumphs, victory and decay, pain and renewal, valleys and mountaintops. It is a peace that unifies your spirit with others. Nevertheless, we cannot and will not experience such an internal peace without the acknowledgement and acceptance of our own value, worth, and personal goodness. Furthermore, we cannot and will not experience this sort of peace until we can wholeheartedly and sincerely accept and love ourselves with unconditional arms.

CHAPTER CHALLENGE: TREE OF THOUGHTS

Try this task when you are struggling with negative or positive thoughts. Imagine that your body, mind, and spirit are a tree, and imagine that your thoughts have been transposed into the tree's leaves and the trunk of the tree. Use this particular task whether your thoughts are negative or positive. The intent of this particular task is to have you openly and candidly express your emotional state. Due to the rat-race mentality of our society, we seldom have time, or make time, to communicate with others, much less our own being; therefore, the emotional condition of our mind is left abandoned. Just for fun, try drawing your own tree. It is an excellent therapeutic exercise that helps stimulate your mind, allowing you to actively express your current mindset.

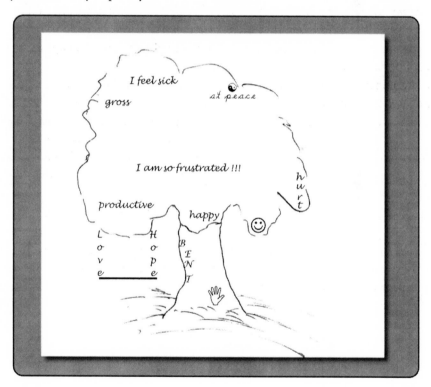

As a guide, following is a list of positive and negative emotions, feelings, and descriptive words. Sometimes it is hard to find the right word to describe your current emotional state. May the following list of words connect you to the right emotional expression.

Abandoned	Abused	Afraid	Aggressive	Agitated
Alarmed	Angry	Anguish	Angst	Annoyed
Anxious	Awesome	Awkward	Beaten	Betrayed
Appalled	Apprehensive	Ashamed	Attacked	Bitter
Blamed	Bothered	Burdened	Butchered	Caught
Cautious	Chaotic	Compelled	Compromised	Conflicted
Concerned	Confused	Constrained	Contempt	Critical
Criticized	Deceived	Defective	Defensive	Dejected
Demoralized	Depressed	Deprived	Deserted	Despair
Desperate	Despondent	Destitute	Devastated	Disadvantaged
Disappointed	Discarded	Discontented	Discouraged	Disgraced
Disgusted	Disheartened	Dishonored	Dismayed	Distraught
Distressed	Disturbed	Doubted	Down	Downhearted
Eager	Earnest	Easy	Edgy	Egregious
Embarrassed	Empty	Enraged	Exacerbated	Exposed
Fake	Favorable	Fearful	Fed up	Fierce
Fired up	Fixed	Flattened	Floored	Fooled
Foolish	Forced	Forlorn	Forsaken	Frightened
Fubsy	Furious	Gloomy	Good	Great
Grief-stricken	Grace	Gratitude	Guilt-ridden	Guilt
Guilty	Handsome	Happy	Harassed	Harmony
Hassled	Hate	Hated	Hatred	Healed
Healthy	Heart	Heartache	Hearty	Heavenly
Heavy	Helpful	Helpless	Here	Holy
Honest	Honored	Hopeless	Horrified	Hug
Huge	Hugged	Humbled	Humiliated	Hurt
Idea	Ideal	Imaginative	Imperfect	Inadequate
Incapable	Incensed	Incomplete	Increase	Incredible
Independent	Infuriated	Ingenious	Innate	Innovate
Insecure	In shock	Instantaneous	Instinct	Insulated
Insulted	Intelligent	Intuitive	Joined	Jovial
Joy	Jubilation	Keen	Keeper	Keyed
Kind	Kindness	Kiss	Knowledgeable	Knowing
Laugh	Leader	Learn	Legendary	Let down
Let go	Light	Limited	Limitless	Lively
Locked	Longing	Looker	Love	Loved
Loveliness	Low	Lucidity	Lucrative	Luminous
Mad	Maintained	Marvelous	Master	Meaningful
Meditative	Melancholy	Metamorphosis	Miserable	Misjudged
Mistreated	Misunderstood	Modified	Motivated	Moving
Nature	Negative	Neglected	Nervous	Nourished
Novel	Now	Nurtured	Nutrition	Obliged
Offended	One	On edge	Open	Openhanded
Optimistic	Outraged	Overwhelmed	Pain	Panic
Panicky	Paradise	Party	Peace	Peaceful
Perfect	Pessimistic	Petrified	Phenomenon	Pity
Pleasure	Plenteous	Plentiful	Plenty	Plethora
Poised	Polished	Popular	Positive	Power
Prepared	Pretty	Proud	Quaint	Quest
Quick	Quiet	Rage	Ready	Recognized
Redundant	Refined	Refreshed	Refused	Rejected
Rejoice	Remarkable	Remorse	Replenished	Resentful

Revered	Sad	Safe	Scared	Scorned
Secure	Sensation	Serenity	Shaken	Shine
Shocked	Silence	Simple	Sincere	Smart
Smile	Smooth	Snubbed	Sponge	Still
Stressed	Team	Tense	Terrified	Tested
Thankful	Threatened	Thrilled	Tormented	Trapped
Troubled	Trusted	Turmoil	Unbalanced	Uncomfortable
Valued	Violated	Visual	Vital	Well
Whole	Willing	Wonderful	Worn	Worried

Relax and Meditate Daily	Journal Your Inner Thoughts	Practice Focused Breathing

CHAPTER NINE

THE PERCEPTIONAL MIND

> Let us fix our attention out of ourselves as much as
> possible; let us chase our imagination to the heavens, or to
> the utmost limits of the universe; we never really advance
> a step beyond ourselves nor can conceive any kind of
> existence but those perceptions which have appeared in
> the narrow compass.
>
> —David Hume

Perception is a sensory tool that allows us to see, hear, and have an awareness of our surroundings. We use our perception to interpret events and situations. Our perceptional mind brings an awareness of our surroundings. Perception has a great deal to do with our ability to unconditionally accept and love ourselves and another. If our perception is dim, then our pathway may be darkened and unclear, and our uncertainty may become heightened. When we are struggling with issues, our perception becomes altered. How we see the world has a lot to do with how we choose to live in the world. If we perceive the world to be a scary place, then we may choose to live life cautiously. You have heard about those who choose to exclude themselves from the rest of the world because of past fears or harm. You may in fact be one of those people, or you may know those who have created virtual or physical shutters to protect themselves from possible harm. Ironically, the fear that has created shutters for security and protection is the same fear that you live with on a daily basis. The fear can physically and psychologically stifle your ability to breathe properly, making life unbearable and undesirable. Our perceptions of the world, of events, and of situations have a great deal to do with how we pursue living life. If we perceive the world to be a continuous adventure, then we may choose to live every moment as though it was our last one to live.

Our perceptional mind has a lot to do with how we pursue life. You may be questioning whether or not it is possible to change your perceptional mind. It is possible to change your perceptional mind, but it takes desire and effort; a conscience awareness of yourself and your surroundings; a sensitivity to your needs versus your wants; and an ambition to live life to its fullest and beyond how you have been living it.

Have you ever heard someone say, "You just don't perceive it the way that I perceive it"? What they are speaking of is the perceptional mind. It is this mind that can guide you down a positive or negative pathway. You train this mind through the information that you take in. Arguably, some information is unconsciously gathered. If we receive information through our unconscious mind, we are processing and making sense of that information as soon as it is received. Although we are not necessarily responsible for unconscious messages, the way we unconsciously interpret these messages lies within the training of our unconscious mind. Have you ever heard the adage, *Garbage in, garbage out?* What this means is that whatever information that is taken inwardly will eventually be expressed outwardly. When was the last time that you consciously considered the thoughts that you were entertaining? Parents, a majority of you are great advocates for promoting good messages. I have rarely heard about a parent allowing their child to sit back and watch a movie promoting racial propaganda, extremely violent acts, or some other negatively geared message.

Why do we protect small children from negative messages or images but do not protect our own minds? Have you ever sat back, waiting for a child to go to bed in order that you might watch a particular show or have a conversation that was for *adult ears only*? Have you ever listened to a colleague tell a sexually driven joke? Have you ever listened to the workplace office gossip, which is more than likely putting down someone or something? Believe it or not, a majority of society has entertained the wrong type of messages. In fact, we are encouraged to listen to negative messages, from Jerry Springer's talk show to the hottest new reality show; we are constantly bombarded by negative messages. Messages, messages, messages. What are the messages that you are entertaining?

Sadly, we give little thought or consideration to the messages that we entertain. We rarely consider the damage that a message may do to our minds. It is rare that parents allow their children to complain about their siblings for the sake of complaining. In most cases, if children come to parents complaining about someone else, we call them a tattletale. Are we not tattletales when we sit back and complain about another? How are our complaints any different from a child's complaints? Are we not essentially doing the same thing or partaking of the same messages? For argument's sake, let's say that adult messages are different and that they do contain some sort of substance beyond simply gossiping or complaining. Are your messages, messages of encouragement? Are your messages promoting and uplifting to another? Or are your messages filled with gossip, complaints, or envy? I have never heard a gossip-filled message that offered something positive. Why is it that a child can be scolded for complaining but we give ourselves allowances, providing us—the adults—the right to complain? I find it sort of comical that we find excuses for our behaviors, attitudes, and beliefs but have little tolerance for negative behavior from others. Recently, I had a teacher who sent me an e-mail message asking for help in her classroom. The teacher discussed having problems with tattletale children and gossip. I asked the teacher how she dealt with the issues. She expressed that she typically gives a child a warning, then—if that doesn't work—places the child in timeout. I discussed with the teacher the importance of hearing out a child, because children are not as good at gauging what is important and what is not important. It is our duty as adults to teach children what is important and what is unimportant. For instance, if a child knows of a situation whereby another child has been hurt, bullied, or harmed, then that child should feel free to inform a teacher, whereas if a child sees another child drawing on the classroom chalkboard, it is not up to the child to report it. In such a case, a child who has reported minor mischief could be viewed as a tattletale. Children should be taught the difference between an important issue versus an unimportant issue. Whereas a child needs to learn this, we hope that adults have already learned to distinguish between important messages and unimportant messages. Have you? Have you learned to distinguish between important messages and unimportant messages? Do you still entertain messages that are negative in their overall content? Are you still apt to gossip or complain about an issue? We give little thought or consideration behind the messages that we entertain. In fact, I have met very few individuals who see negative messages as a problem.

Let's look at negative messages with a different perceptional mindset. What if you were overweight? What if every single day you were to eat six or seven candy bars, drink a six-pack of pop, and have a gallon of ice cream to finish off your meal? Would this have an effect? Of course it would have a negative effect on your body. Even if you were working out rigorously every day, it would have a negative effect on your body. Although most people do not have such a diet, they have adopted a destructive habit of inviting negative messages and perceptions into their psychological and spiritual being. Taking negative messages in will have the same effect on your spiritual and psychological being as having a poorly designed diet. Negative messages are digested similar to how food is processed and ultimately decomposed. We receive the messages through our eyes, ears, or thoughts. We digest the message, sending the message to our mind to process, distribute, contemplate, and finally break down the content of that message like enzymes do in the human digestive tract to distribute throughout our being. You may be asking yourself, "What do you mean that we distribute negative messages throughout our bodies?" You may even feel that negative messages have no effect on your body. Let me ask you a question: Have you ever been so stressed out because of a situation that you have a headache, neck ache, backache, or stomachache? Have you lay awake at night dwelling on an event, situation, or circumstance that happened the previous day? Have you struggled with a thought? If so, you have been negatively affected by negative messages.

Have you ever watched an hour of television? How many infomercials do you see promoting some sort of health-oriented agenda? I bet you see commercials promoting diet, fitness, and physical health. However, it is a rare day that you or I would see an advertisement concerning a positive lifestyle, especially an advertisement discussing how to improve your psychological or spiritual being that did not involve some sort of medication. Sadly, a majority of the advertisements on television discussing your psychological health are commercials promoting some newly formed medication. Have you ever listened to these commercials? I must admit that when I hear such commercials, I want to run for the hills to escape the negative effect of most medications. The side effects of most modern-day psychiatric and psychological-based medications are frightening. I am not advocating against such medications, because medications do have their time and place. However, as a private practitioner, I can tell you that so many of my patients are either overly medicated, or medicated for insignificant issues or for the wrong reasons. Medications will not and cannot change negative messages of your past. Medications will not change your history. Nor will medications make you more popular or desirable. Medications are not capable of repairing a bad relationship or bad thoughts. You, as an individual, must make the changes that you so desire. You must put forth the effort to make the changes that you wish to have in your life. Just as with a diet pill, as a society, we are seeking out the right pill to control our thoughts, but—in reality—you and I are responsible for every single thought that we entertain. We create excuses so that we don't have to accept responsibility. We avoid being responsible by laying blame at someone else's doorstep. We have become an excuse-oriented society. There is no escaping, however, that we are ultimately responsible for our thoughts, deeds, actions, and reactions.

What if you were blind? Do you think and feel that you would be nearly as concerned about or concentrated on your physical looks or the physical appearance of another? How would your blindness change your perspective of the world? What if your blindness occurred later in life? Would your previous sight change the way you now see the world? How would you adapt to your blindness? What would your perception of self be now due to how you now see others?

Let's take it one step further: What if you were deaf? How would this affect the way you see yourself and others? Would it? Have you ever met someone whose tone of voice did not mesh with your perception of their physical appearance? How did this impact your perception of that person? Did it? Were you capable of communicating with that person? How did you expect this individual's voice to sound? Can you describe it? Did you have a preset idea of the voice's tone or pitch, or the frequency with which they would speak? Were you capable of seeing the person and his or her voice as a synonymous entity? Have you ever been told that your voice does not match your physical appearance? How did it impact you? How did you respond?

What if you were both deaf and blind; how would this change how you perceive others? Would it change the way you communicate with others? Of course it would change how you communicate with others, or would it? Why are our perceptions so ingrained? What can cause our perceptions to be altered? Our perception can be altered by a host of events. It can be affected by verbal communication and physical situations, and our perception can be altered for the negative and the positive. It is possible to intentionally change your perception. Our perceptions can be consciously and unconsciously affected. The effects of our past can alter our perceptions. As children, we are taught by our parents, teachers, religious leaders, and others what to believe, how to believe it, and why we should believe. Our beliefs have a direct effect on our perceptions.

Do you dream? When you are experiencing a dream, can you distinguish between your reality and the dream? Dreams are a pathway into our perceptional mind. They can take us back to a past memory or an event. They can cause us to relive a pain or sorrow as well as a triumph or victory. Dreams can bring our attention to needs and tasks that should be accomplished, and remind us of tasks that we forgot to achieve. They can encourage us, motivate us, and reinforce our life's ambitions. Martin Luther King, Jr., had a mental dream, an aspiration that one day all humankind would experience equality. Dreams can be an inspiration, or they can detour us from achieving our greatest desires. Our dreams have influence over our perceptions, and our perceptions have influence over our dreams. Without our physical dreams and our psychological ambitions, we would avoid pursuing, inviting, inspiring, or fulfilling our life's ambitions. Our dreams are altered by our perceptions, and our perceptions can be altered by our dreams.

CHAPTER CHALLENGE: **CHANGING OUR**
                               PERCEPTIONAL MIND

This particular set of exercises has been designed to challenge your perceptions. It might be interesting to do these exercises with friends, family, and colleagues. You should journal about each experience, reviewing them at a later time and place. Be certain to read through the rules of each task before proceeding.

1.) Go outside today, have a seat, then close your eyes for a few minutes. After having your eyes closed for several minutes, open them. How does the world appear to you? Has it changed? Write about this experience:

2.) Go to a mall with friends to play peek-a-boo. What were people's verbal responses? What was your perception of their nonverbal language? How did it feel to be playing peek-a-boo with someone other than a toddler or infant? Did you feel embarrassed? Why? Write about this experience:

3.) If you have access to two sinks, fill one sink with cool water and the other sink with warm water. Place your hand in warm water. After a minute or so, remove your hand from the warm water and place it into the cold water. What was your immediate reaction? How did you respond?

4.) Begin by having someone hold two pencils gently in the center of your back. Have them hold the pencils in the center of your back for 3 to 4 minutes. Without them telling you, have them remove the pencils. Were you aware of the pencils being removed? What was the sensation of having the pencils placed on your back? Write about this experience:

Relax and Meditate Daily	Journal Your Inner Thoughts	Practice Focused Breathing

CHAPTER TEN

ALTERING OUR MINDS, ALTERING OUR PERCEPTION

> It is not important what happens to you, but how you perceive what happens to you.
>
> —Stephen Convey

You can change your perception. Changing your perception takes effort, desire, purpose, and intent. We all have pasts; how we perceive the past influences our present. You have probably met someone, or perhaps you know someone, who lives in the past. You yourself may have had times when you chose to reside in your own past. The past, this historical reminder of our lives, can plague us like a bad case of indigestion. Have you ever noticed that indigestion tends to be most pronounced when you are stressed? Our negative past is not much different; it seems to be the most pronounced when we are under the most deal of stress. In fact, isn't it ironic how your past seems to come to the forefront of your mind when you are stressed? Not unlike indigestion, our past and our perceptions can be changed. "What?" you may be asking, "How can *I* change my past?" You may even be saying to yourself, "You fool, there is no way that you can change or alter your past. That's why it's called the *past*." I realize that we cannot physically change acts, deeds, situations, or events in our past, but we can without a doubt change how we perceive our past.

Our perceptional mind is capable of being changed. We can change our perceptional mind through positive reinforcements. The reinforcements act as an instrument of support, strengthening our perceptional mind. Our perceptional mind is an awareness of our surroundings. It is through our perceptional mind that we can hear, see, and think, becoming attentive to our perceptional senses. Our perceptional mind is made up of organic matter, cognitive processing, neurological pathways, a psychological self, and the indwelling of our spirit. Therefore, it is important that we are in charge of our body. Otherwise, the makeup of our body and its perceptional mind can become an instrument of chaos. Gaining control of your perceptional mind is not a difficult task. The perceptional mind is one of the least attended components of the human condition. People rarely give thought to what enters their perceptional mind. It is seldom that we sit back and monitor information being discussed. The exception occurs when there are children present or those whom we revere or seek to impress.

Gaining control of our perceptional mind takes physical, mental, and spiritual exertion. At first, we may struggle gaining control over our perceptional minds, but in time, like any other form of exercise, we will become masters of our destiny and our perceptional minds.

Do not forget that a great deal of the difficulties with perceptional mind occurs because it is not properly reinforced. What happens if a house is built with weak beams? In time, the house will prove an engineering nightmare, and it may eventually collapse. Similarly, if our perceptional minds are built with weak or negative reinforcements, then our personal being will eventually decay, allowing for only a shell of our true person to exist. The spiritual person suffers as well, because if you are not working on your perceptional mind, you have weakened the overall structure of your being.

Reinforcing our perceptional mind occurs when we take charge of our being. Have you ever had an opportunity to watch the movie "Life is Beautiful"? It is a movie inspired about the life of a Jewish Italian who becomes a prisoner in a Nazi internment camp during World War II. The primary character, Guido, played by Roberto Benigni, tries his best to keep his family together while being held captive in an internment camp. Guido struggles to protect his son from enduring the hardship and negativity associated with war. He devises a plan to make the experience a mere game using his wit, charm, and intelligence. He not only brings beauty to a very dark place for his son, but he adds beauty to the lives of others who are enduring the same hardship. Guido's passion and unconditional love for his son are clearly evident through his desire to protect his son's innocence and perceptions from being altered by the cruelties of war.

How are you protecting your perceptional mind? Are you adding life and beauty to the perceptional minds of those around you? What are you doing to ensure that the world is filled with beauty, love, and passion? Are you engaging in thoughts, deeds, and actions that nullify the beauty that exists in your life? Or are you seeking ways to foster the beauty and love within you? Our perceptions are influenced by our surroundings. We can either choose to engage in negativity or seek out the positive in life. We can educate our minds and the minds around us with positive information, or we can be influencers of decay and harm. What drives and motivates you? What are your perceptional values? Are you stuck in a rut of negativity? Have you become stagnate and filled with negativity? If so, let's bring life to you and those around you. Let's make your world a better place to live. Let's have others say that you brought beauty to this sometimes dark world.

CHAPTER CHALLENGE: **PERCEPTIONS**

In the following challenge, there are two images. Focus on these two images for one minute.

What are your perceptions of the images?

Which image is your mind immediately drawn to?

What does your mind choose to see?

What have you programmed your mind to perceive?

Try this as an additional exercise: Focus on the two images for a minute. Next, shift your eyes to a blank wall. What occurs? What do you perceive?

Many have trained their minds to see the dark circle on the right. Others may see the white circle. Research has shown that our minds are trained to think, believe, and perceive life relative to the way we think. Our perceptions may be drawn to the dark figure because of negative energy, whereas, we may have trained our mind to see the light figure as positive. However, the truth is that darkness does not always have to represent bleakness, nor does light always have to represent goodness. The truth can be reversed for you, depending on how you have trained your perceptional mind to see these shades. Likewise, when we encounter negativity, our minds are either drawn to overcome the negativity or drawn into the negativity. It depends on our perceptions of negativity whether we will choose to follow a negative path or a positive one. Either way, we are responsible for choosing how we interpret perceptional data in our lives. Shaping our perceptions occurs through conscious and unconscious efforts.

Just for fun, try viewing and making sense out of the following images.

Which one of these two figures is correct? Why?

Our perceptional mind informs us how we should interpret an object. It informs us whether an object is right-side-up or upside down. It informs us whether an object has all of the correct pieces or whether an object is missing pieces. Therefore, the perceptual mind deciphers what is wrong and what is right, providing us with an explanation of how to correct the image.

What do you see in this picture?

Do you see the silhouettes of two people?
Do you see the candlestick?

If so, then you have visually given meaning to a mismatch of figures. The science behind our visual perceptions is what we call optical illusions. An optical illusion is what occurs when an object is perceived to be a particular way, but the reality is that the object is a bundle of visual mismatches making up a visual idea or concept.

Relax and Meditate Daily	Journal Your Inner Thoughts	Practice Focused Breathing

CHAPTER ELEVEN

THE BLAME AND SHAME GAME

You can never cross the ocean unless you have the courage
to lose sight of the shore.

—Christopher Columbus

Are you drawn to the issues in your past? Do you know someone that
reminds you of your past mistakes? Why is it that you feel compelled to
allow your mind to wander down life's destructive highways? In my life,
I have known many good people who have made mistakes, as we all do,
but allow these errors to consume the remainder of their life. I, too, have
made many mistakes, but one valuable lesson that I have learned is that
we cannot allow our mistakes to become our identity. It is necessary that
we learn from our mistakes, accept the responsibility of those mistakes,
and move our lives forward. If we allow our past to consume our present
thoughts, then we have allowed the past to rule our lives. When we allow
our past to be our present, we are allowing ourselves to become captives of
that past. What would you do if you knew of a loved one that could not
forgive themselves for past deeds? Would you encourage that loved one to
stay in the virtual negative cinema of their past, replaying and repeating
the negative reels of their past? Or would you encourage that loved one
to move forward from their past? Let's look at it in a different context.
Have you ever known someone who constantly reminded you of all of
their successes in this life? What if this person constantly kept repeating
this on a daily basis, living life based on their past successes? What would
be your response? Most people would see this individual from a negative
perspective. In many cases, individuals who announce their successes
are looked down on, whereas individuals who announce their failures are
shown pity. Why is it that we find a need to either share our past with
others or remind ourselves of our past? It is because we are choosing to live
in the past rather than work on our present state of being. Ask yourself the
next time you announce or think about past successes or failures, "Why
am I seeking approval and acceptance?"

When we live in the past, we are seeking to place blame and shame on others or our own person. Living in a state of blame and shame is much like being placed in a maximum security jail cell. You are a captive of the issues in your past. You are not proving a victor of this life. Did you know that you can be bombarded by past negative and positive memories of this life? Did you know that there are individuals who become stuck in their theaters of despair, heartache, disappointments, and errors of life? Did you also know that, not unlike the virtual loop of negative cinema, you can become a captive of your positive cinema as well? When we achieve greatness in this life, we sometimes feel as though we have experienced life to its fullest; therefore, our future abilities to live life become unattainable. If you live according to your past successes, then you are living life no differently from the person who lives life according to their past failures. When we seek out blame and shame, or seek to place blame and shame, we are living in the past. Did you know that you can place blame and shame on your successes? Have you ever heard anyone complain about the pleasures of success? Have you ever known anyone who says, "You just don't understand the demands that come with success"? Are they living in the present moment? Are they living life abundantly? Most assuredly not; if you have disdain for your successes, you have become roped into the blame and shame game.

What is the blame and shame game? Have you ever sought someone or something to blame for the condition of your life? Have you ever blamed yourself for the condition of your life? Do you feel discouraged and shameful about your past? Have others made you feel ashamed for past errors in life? If so, you are playing the blame and shame game. Our lives and our identity are not about what we have done right or wrong. The lives of those around us should not influence the way we see ourselves, but when we allow our past experiences in this life to influence the way we see ourselves, we choose to live in the past. Likewise, if you choose to live in the past, you are living in a state of blame and shame. Whether you feel personal shame for deeds you have done or you blame another, your life will not be lived abundantly until you can allow your past to become history.

What have you done wrong in your life that continues to plague you? Have you made some egregious error in this life that you feel is unforgivable? If you have someone of importance in this life, perhaps a child, are you capable of loving this person unconditionally? What if this person made a truly negative mistake in his or her life? Would your love for them falter, going by the wayside? What would it take for you to stop loving another individual? If you love someone unconditionally, including yourself, you cannot live in the past. Unconditional love knows neither our good deeds nor our bad ones. Unconditional love looks beyond our human errors and mistakes, and sees us as our spirit. If our identity is our spirit and not our human flesh, then the mistakes and errors we make in this life have no bearing on our perception of self or others. If we unconditionally love ourselves, we unconditionally love others, seeing them beyond their past. If we unconditionally love ourselves and another, we cannot contain within our minds the deeds of the past. Therefore, we are incapable of containing shame or blame in our minds or spirits. Shame and blame should have no place in our body, mind, or spirit.

If our perception is that we are bad, then we are holding on to shame and blaming ourselves for something in our past. Yes, our past. You may be saying to yourself, "My past has nothing to do with the way that I see myself today." You may also be thinking of your past as something days, weeks, or months ago, but the reality is that your past was a breath ago. If you consider the basic concept of breathing in relationship to your past, then for each breath you take, you have had additional pasts. Each breath that exits your lungs is like a driving force of energy shedding off another moment, adding to your past.

CHAPTER CHALLENGE: **PLAYING THE BLAME**
                                          AND SHAME GAME

In our lives, we have encountered situations that we have all—yes, all—
sought to lay blame for. You may be thinking to yourself, "Not me. I am
always responsible for my actions." Let me give you a few examples of
laying blame: "They made me do it"; "The dog ate my assignment"; "It
wasn't my fault; everyone else was doing it too"; "I was only borrowing a
few supplies. After all, the office owes me." These are pure excuses that
equate to total blame. Seeking blame is like seeking out someone else to
be responsible for your actions. Be responsible, accept your responsibility,
and proceed to live life abundantly.

Think back on your life. Have you ever blamed someone else for your
negative behavior? If so, you too have played the blame and shame game.
There are many ways to blame others for your behaviors as well as to
accept blame, or shame. This is your mission, if you care to accept it: We
are going to pretend for a moment that you are a therapist. Imagine that
you have had two patients enter your office arguing about who is to blame
for something. Here is your job: You are to decide how to help these two
individuals accept their own responsibility for the discord.

The couple is arguing. They are blaming each other for being late for their
therapeutic appointment. The wife says that her husband was supposed
to set the alarm clock, and the husband says that his wife was supposed
to remind him to set it. The wife is emotional and perhaps irrational, and
the husband appears distant and indifferent to the situation. It is up to
you to help guide this couple to a healthy solution.

1.) As a therapist, you

   a) side with the wife because she is expressing emotions
   b) side with the husband because he is *over it*
   c) side with neither because it appears that there was a breach in
       communication

2.) As a therapist, you have heard the dispute. You

   a) tell the husband that he is being cold, indifferent, and without
       emotion

b) express to the wife that she is being overly sensitive and that she should get over herself

c) express to both the wife and husband that they may have some shared responsibility

3.) As a therapist, you are getting frustrated with the flow of the conversation. You

a) are allowing their behaviors to influence your own behaviors

b) display a positive behavior because they should respect your role as a therapist

c) should be frustrated because they are wasting your time as a professional

4.) As a therapist, you guide the couple to finding a healthy solution. An example of a healthy solution might be

a) tell the couple to forgive and forget because they will never resolve the dispute

b) tell the couple to forgive and forget because neither are right

c) tell the couple to forgive and forget because there is no benefit in being right or wrong

In your role as therapist, you may have found it difficult to answer the previous questions. You may have found yourself bouncing back and forth between answers. If you chose the following answers, you are well on your way to understanding responsibility:

1.) C - In life, a dispute may arise because a lack of communication has occurred. When miscommunication occurs, understand that neither person was seeking to wrong the other, rather understand that life sometimes encounters hiccups.

2.) C - In some cases, you may have shared responsibility in an error in communication. Understand that it is alright to be wrong, because when we are wrong, (a perceptional failure), we have an opportunity for personal growth.

3.) A - As a therapist and as a person, you may encounter a situation whereby others are disagreeing. Not much different from their personal dispute, you too have a responsibility to maintain your composure.

4.) C - In life, a dispute may arise that there are no absolute answers, don't seek to be right or wrong, but seek to resolve the dispute with a mutual understanding that we may simply agree to disagree.

Did you know that you are a therapist? Everyone plays the role of therapist at some point in their lives. You may find yourself providing counsel to your children, a spouse, a life partner, a colleague, a business partner, a boss, a friend, a family member, or some other significant person in your life. As a therapist, you can be certain that you will not always hit home runs. As a therapist, you may make errors in judgments, but do not be dismayed. We all make mistakes, and mistakes are part of the growth cycle. Without mistakes, we would have nothing to improve on. It is always important to look at each situation with unbiased lenses or eyes. Next time this occurs, try looking for solutions that are unbiased. Try having those involved in the dispute reconcile before the end of the day. Did you know that, in most cases, disputes that are unresolved can transform into lifelong hostilities? It is vitally important to resolve all disputes before laying your head down for the night.

Relax and Meditate Daily	Journal Your Inner Thoughts	Practice Focused Breathing

CHAPTER TWELVE

PERSONAL RESPONSIBILITY

You must take personal responsibility. You cannot change
the circumstances, the seasons, or the wind, but you can
change yourself. That is something you have charge of.

—Jim Rohn

Many years ago, I had the distinct honor of working with a couple of
mentally handicapped individuals. I loved it. My work was rewarding,
educating, and in so many ways refreshing. My time with these individuals
taught me about so many aspects of life. I look back on this experience
with sincere and heartfelt fondness. I gained a renewed image of what
humankind was all about, and a greater understanding of the human
spirit. It was through my work with these individuals that I first gained
insight into the concepts *self-control* and *personal choices*. Although these
individuals had a variety of physical and mental challenges, I learned
that they, too, were responsible for their own actions. It became clear
that they were responsible for their choices, habits, and decision-making
processes. If they chose to do something wrong, it was no different than
you and I choosing to engage in something that was wrong. If they
chose something that was productive for their lives, then they were also
responsible for making such choices. There are some individuals who
function at lower intellectual quotients (IQs) than others, but this does
not diminish their ability or capacity to make decisions and choices in
life. Ironically, like so many others, I had a prefabricated idea of mentally
handicapped individuals. In fact, this learning curve taught me that even
if you have a physical disability, a mental disability, or any other disability
that limits a perspective of your life, you remain capable of making choices.
We all make choices. Whether or not they are clearly understood by others
is for another discussion, but it is apparent that we can all make choices of
our own understanding and comprehension.

This learning curve was a true and genuinely mind-awakening experience.
It was a personal epiphany. In fact, this awakening occurred beyond my
human mind; it affected my spiritual mind as well. Please understand that

I am not saying that I never made a mistake; rather, it was when I became aware of the concept of *personal responsibility*. Personal responsibility is the ability to take ownership of what we have intentionally or unintentionally done wrong or right. Personal responsibility is taking the initiative to assess, accept, and seek out measures to resolve or improve a situation that may have been created by our own person. It does not mean that we have failed or have become unworthy. Rather, it shows that we are willing to accept a situation for what it has become and have a desire to improve it. We have intentionally or unintentionally created the problem; it is now our responsibility to accept it, resolve it, and move forward.

If we perceive something as a personal failure, or that we are failures as a result of a situation, then we are creating additional harm to ourselves. Furthermore, any harm that we create for ourselves, we project outwardly, causing additional harm. We are not designed to carry around blame or shame. Blame and shame are simply mind games. We are not designed to think on the negative or take ownership of it. Shame and blame are not something that we should seek out and carry in a basket like an Easter egg being sought out by a child. There is no room for embarrassment, either, for if we take personal responsibility, we deny the right to place shame on ourselves, project blame on another, or allow embarrassment to creep into our lives. Shame, blame, and embarrassment offer nothing of substance to our lives or the lives of others. Shame, blame, and embarrassment are like high LDL (low-density lipoprotein) cholesterol. They can slowly accumulate in the body's arteries, negatively clogging the passages through which positive information flows. In time, constant negative information will accumulate to the point that it clogs your mental and physical pathways so that you become numb and indifferent, ultimately decaying and potentially dying as a human.

My work with the handicapped population taught me a great deal about myself, others, and the human species in general. They taught me that I should not feel fear when accepting personal responsibility. You might be asking yourself, "Why would you have felt fear around accepting personal responsibility?" You may even think to yourself that you could accept personal responsibility without reservation or hesitation. Moreover, you may even be pondering why anyone could not feel safe in sharing, accepting, or acknowledging responsibility for their own deeds, whether intentional or unintentional. Of course, we could go through many names in the world of politics, Hollywood, Bollywood, and religious circles that have chosen not to take personal responsibility. The numbers are vast, and it seems that the media continuously reminds us of their names, deeds, and actions. It is truly sad that we as humans cannot let go of others' past much less our own. Here, again, we are brought back to the shame and blame game. We are constantly witnessing others choosing not to accept personal responsibility. They seek out ways to deflect responsibility or redirect responsibility to another. We hear of countless tales of how someone chose to lie and hide from the truth to avoid yet another case of embarrassment.

Personal responsibility is the willingness to completely accept choices that we have made throughout our life. It is the responsibility of you, the owner of your thoughts, deeds, and actions, to make choices that follow your own personal ethical and moral system of belief. Accepting personal responsibility is not a burden; it is a freedom, it is liberating, and it is necessary to live life abundantly. Personal responsibility is not the acceptance of others' bad or good deeds. How can I accept the positive deeds of my daughter? If my daughter puts forth the effort to make good grades, then it is my daughter's responsibility to accept recognition for those accomplishments. If I help my daughter with her studies, then I can accept some of the credit for her skillful development as a student and a person. Personal responsibility is not based on blame, shame, or guilt. It has nothing to do with accepting responsibility for others' choices.

As a therapist, I have heard countless stories describing personal victimization. Accepting personal responsibility is not an indication that you must forgive and forget. It has nothing to do with your victimizer; rather, it has to do with your ability to thrive and to live beyond a simple state of survival. For so many, when they are traumatized, they let the moment of traumatization define them. You are not a victim but rather an individual who has incurred a victimization. A person who accepts personal responsibility will not allow themselves to be defined by their victimization. Instead, you accept that you have been victimized, and you make choices to live a life beyond this victimization. Accepting personal responsibility says, "I will not allow you or anyone else that I know to victimize me." Furthermore, it says, "I will not allow you or anyone else to victimize another person or creature." Personal responsibility goes beyond the state of victimization, making you responsible for the remainder of your life. Your life does not have to be defined by a situation, event, or another person. You can live life and live it abundantly.

In life, we may face a variety of hardships, trials, tribulations, and challenges. It is the acceptance that you are the captain and commander of your life that will ultimately be the guide map of your life. Whether you have lost your job because of a depression, recession, or some unforeseen economic turn, accepting personal responsibility for your life helps you to lash up your shoes and move forward. Your home may have been destroyed by a flood, fire, or some other natural force of nature. Do not allow this event to define or devastate your life. Imagine if you lived in a wild frontier. Imagine that your nearest neighbor lived nearly 500 miles away. What would you do if your home was destroyed by a tree that had collapsed due to a strong wind or storm? What are your instincts telling you at this very moment? Would you give up and find refuge in your neighbor's home? What if, you were incapable of traveling to your closest neighbor's home? Then what? Would you continue to make excuses or find excuses behind your inability to thrive at your location? Please do not misunderstand me; natural disasters are an unimaginable occurrence. But what would you do if your life was altered because of a natural disaster? Accepting personal responsibility is looking at a situation and realizing you must make the most out of what life has offered you at a particular time and place.

You are not the product of your environment or your physiological creation. Who you are has nothing to do with how you were created; it has to do with how you respond to this life, its challenges, and its rewards. Let's look at an example of personal responsibility: The late actor Christopher Reeve had a blossoming career full of hope, possibilities, and choices. On May 27, 1995, Christopher Reeve was thrown from a horse while competing in an equestrian event. Mr. Reeve's life would drastically change due to this fateful day. He would no longer have the ability to walk, much less ride a horse competitively. Mr. Reeve's choices from that day forward would not only impact his own life but the lives of many others who had incurred the effects of a spinal cord injury. With his global influence, Mr. Reeve pursued many avenues that would test not only the field of science but the community at large. His own personal pursuits would challenge the science behind spinal cord injuries, human embryonic stem cell research, and those with a variety of disabilities. Although Mr. Reeve's body transformed from one of a capable, highly functioning adult into an adult with many physical challenges, he would not allow it to prove a detriment to his internal spirit to thrive on this earth. Mr. Reeve's unwillingness to allow this event to become his Achille's heel forced others to see their physical disabilities as personal challenges rather than the end of their lives. Mr. Reeve went beyond simply seeking a cure for his own injuries; he established the Christopher & Dana Reeve Foundation to research treatments and cures for paralysis of all kinds. "I have always been a crusader for causes I believe in. This time, the cause found me," Mr. Reeve was quoted as saying. While it was his own personal injury that brought his attention to the issue of paralysis, it was through Mr. Reeve's own personal effort to survive that people were encouraged to watch a man slowly transform his body back into a body of capability, possibility, and hope. Although Mr. Reeve's new life ambition to walk again would never be realized, his spirit continues to run free like a horse galloping through a field of wheat and barley.

A life-changing injury was a turning point for Mr. Reeve. Mr. Reeve would not settle for *I can't*. Rather, he accepted his plight, took the reigns of personal responsibility, and haltered it despite his personal challenges. He allowed himself to live life through his challenges. It was through his willingness to accept his challenges that he was capable of becoming an incredible force of change. Mr. Reeve's life challenged humanity to look at many dynamics of individuals facing paralysis. He drew attention to the plight of those faced with a variety of challenges, encouraging the global scientific community to develop new sciences and refresh old sciences. He redefined his own life by making his goal to walk, something most individuals take for granted. He allowed his daily routine and challenges to be a televised event, encouraging others with challenges. He chose not to see himself as someone who was disabled but rather as someone with a challenge to live and to live life abundantly. Mr. Reeve did not become a product of his environment or situation, but saw this as an opportunity to live life to its fullest. Whether you are someone who is facing a similar situation to Mr. Reeve's or you have another type of challenge, I encourage you to look at your situation merely as a challenge. I also encourage you to accept your personal responsibility to make the most out of your life despite the challenges facing you.

What challenges have been presented to you in this life? Are you facing your own challenges head on or from behind a wall of denial? Challenges are not always laid at our feet in a negative package. Sometimes challenges can be presented in a positive package as well. For example, what if you had always struggled with financial debt, but one day you receive a knock at your door? What if behind that door stood a man who offered you some sort of financial liberation? What if this financial liberation could free you from all of your debt, your children's debts, and their children's debts? How would you respond? What would be the impact of this challenge on your life? How would you choose to live life at this point?

Whether you are faced with challenges that are positive or negative, do not allow these challenges to define you. You are capable of making choices in your life. Remember that your choices may elevate you or break you. So how are you going to respond to the challenges presented in your life? Are you willing to make healthy choices or negative ones? Will you accept your own personal responsibility or reject it? Even if you have been born with physical challenges, psychiatric or psychological challenges, or other challenges, you are capable of making choices for the direction of your life. You may have been a child of abuse, neglect, or maltreatment, but it is up to you to make the choice to live beyond your past. You are not your past, nor can you be defined by your past. You may allow yourself and others to use this as the definition of you, but it is up to you—the author of your life—to accept responsibility for your life.

We are not responsible for choices made by others. If our child chooses to disobey us, we are not responsible for their behavioral outburst. Likewise, if our child chooses to follow a positive pathway in life, we are not responsible for those choices, either. You may be asking yourself, "What if I encouraged my child to make the right choice?" Although you may have encouraged your child to follow a particular pathway, no one can be forced to make choices beyond their personal desires. Have you ever had a situation in which a young child is unwilling to comply with a particular set of directions? What did you do? How did you encourage the child to see the situation from your own perspective? Were you capable of encouraging the child to see it your way? Why, or why not? It is important to recognize that no one—that is correct, no one—can be forced to follow a particular pathway. You may be asking yourself, "What if I was a part of the military and my commanders demanded that I follow a particular set of instructions, even if these instructions went against my own moral code of ethics?" Well, then, you have a decision to make: Will you follow a commander's demands or follow the higher moral route? You can and have the ability to make choices contrary to the authorities in your life. But, you think to yourself, you will be prosecuted, charged, disciplined, or fired. Is it not more important to be a person of high moral character with an ethical backbone than to follow an order that goes against your moral and ethical belief system?

We have the right to deny personal responsibility. However, if we choose to deny personal responsibility for matters that we have clear and undeniable ownership, then it only delays the inevitable, the inevitable being the truth. There are people who have robbed banks, stolen from a cookie jar, borrowed a book with the intent not to return it, or taken a pencil from work thinking, "Well, the office can supply my goods." There are people who intentionally harm others and perceivably get away with it, but know this—they don't. For even if they never speak one word of it, if they never are found guilty in a court of law, they will carry these deeds with them until they have chosen to resolve them if only within their own mind. Taking personal responsibility begins within us. If I lie to you, then I am also lying to myself, but if I look into that mirror and accept responsibility, then I have begun my recovery to health, balance, and well-being. Moreover, if we deny, deflect, or redirect responsibility, we have only delayed the knowledge of these events to be unveiled at another point in time. It is important that you understand that I am not suggesting that you go out and shout from your gut the most egregious deeds that you have committed. In fact, I suggest that you begin within your own being before starting the process of reconciliation with others. Once you forgive yourself of your transgressions, if you feel a need or a call to discuss or ask forgiveness from another, then you should weigh the good that could come from uncovering these issues. In some cases, you may be incapable of sharing the issues that you have had with someone that you feel you have wronged. If so, do not fret, for it is the intent of your heart that matters. Only when you can forgive yourself can you honestly ask another to forgive you. Likewise, it is rare that someone who has not sought internal forgiveness can think of taking on the full responsibility or ownership of deeds they have committed.

Consider the following: Each negative deed, action, or thought is designated a separate bag. What if you were to carry these bags around while denying their existence? They would begin to take a toll on your body, your mind, and your spirit. These bags do not have to be known by anyone else, but it is crucial to understand that these bags will remain in the lockers of your mind until you purge them. How long are you intending on closeting these bags? Are you running out of room? What if you decided to go on a trip to, say, a foreign destination. Then what—are you going to carry every single bag that you have had stored in your virtual closet? Ridding yourself of these bags is to ask forgiveness of yourself and accept personal responsibility. If you rid yourself of these bags, then you have conquered the fear of embarrassment, shame, and blame. However, if you continue to deny these issues, you are continuing to deny, deflect, or redirect your personal responsibility and ownership of these situations. If you desire to become a person capable of experiencing happiness on a continuum, you must be capable of taking on personal responsibility and the ownership therein. If you choose not to, you will carry these issues around with you throughout your life until they are resolved. I am not suggesting that you necessarily contact people that you have wronged after weeks, months, or years have gone by, but if you feel drawn to do so, be certain that you have accepted responsibility within your own mind, ultimately bringing yourself towards peace.

CHAPTER CHALLENGE: THE POWER OF ACCEPTING RESPONSIBILITY

Responsibility is a scary proposition. You may feel judged, condemned, unworthy, questioned, and a host of other emotional responses to an event, situation, or circumstance whereby you have failed to prove your ultimate best. As humans, we are bound to make mistakes. We will make mistakes, and in some cases the mistakes are out of our control, but accepting responsibility is something within our control. Our society has become one that condemns with an iron fist. We fear the repercussions of our mistakes because of the fear of disappointing others or ourselves. We also fear the judgments often cast by others because of our mistakes. Naturally, as in any situation, our human tendency is to fight back or flee the situation. We should fully accept our mistakes, repairing what needs repair, and moving forward with our lives. The greatest difficulty stems from identifying with your human errors, the realization that you are not your mistakes, and that there should be no correlation made between you and your mistakes. It can be difficult to accept responsibility, but accepting it will allow the healing process to begin immediately. Don't get me wrong; there will be some who choose to continue carrying around the message of your mistakes, but for you, if you want to live a life free of your mistakes, you must initially forgive yourself, then seek out those you have wronged. It will not be easy, but it is necessary if you want to live life abundantly.

Accepting responsibility is not only associated with our mistakes. In some cases, we may find it difficult to accept responsibility for the positive areas of our life, too.

Responsibility is the admission that you have a role in this game called life. It is important that you do not identify with the good or bad in your life. You are not your successes or your failures.

Blame and shame create bondage to your mistakes, therefore denying you the right to live a life of happiness and peace. If you accept responsibility, you are accepting the leadership role of your life. By accepting the leadership role, you are denying others the right to have power over your ability to live life abundantly.

Begin each day by saying a positive affirmation in the mirror. The following is an example of a positive affirmation.

Mirror Assignment

I am a person of worth.

I am a person of value.

I am a person deserving of respect, love, and kindness.

I am a person deserving of friendships and relationships.

I am a person made up of my human mind, body, and spirit.

FORGIVENESS

Have you ever heard of someone holding onto a grudge for years, perhaps for several decades? Do you know someone who has held onto anger for years? Have you ever been outraged, displeased, offended, annoyed, irritated, aggravated, provoked, or angry due to another's actions? Have you ever felt as though you had done someone wrong, but failed to ask their forgiveness? Have you ever offended someone? What is it like to carry the burden of unresolved issues? Can you forgive others of their shortcomings? Are you capable of forgiving yourself of your own shortcomings? Forgiveness has been discussed, taught, proclaimed, requested, debated, initiated, and regurgitated time and time again. It is the fundamental knowledge of forgiveness that so many desire but never fully experience. Forgiveness is relatively simple. If I have offended, displeased, annoyed, irritated, aggravated, provoked, or angered another or myself, then I owe the other or myself to ask forgiveness. In an ideal world, we would be capable of asking every single person we have ever harmed for their hand in forgiveness. However, the world is not always ideal and we will not always have an opportunity to apologize to others. Therefore, if you are incapable of asking forgiveness of some, it is always wise that you forgive yourself. Asking forgiveness can prove humbling, but it is necessary. What if I am unable to ask another to forgive me? Then it is important that you speak the words that you would have shared with that other person. Forgiveness does not always have to be met with a face-to-face encounter. Likewise, forgiveness must be experienced within you, for real forgiveness cannot occur until you forgive yourself.

Did you know that studies have revealed that those who have learned to forgive live happier, healthier, and more satisfying lives?

Dr. Fred Luskin is one of many researchers who have shown the necessity of forgiveness. Forgiveness is a learned behavior and the opposite of it is learned, also. So, are you capable of forgiving? Do you have a desire to forgive?

Forgiveness must be initiated before life can begin.

Have you received forgiveness?

Do you desire forgiveness?

Did you know that if you hold on to past wrongs that they can become initiators of health difficulties, concerns, and disorders?

Are you hanging onto anger from long ago?

How would it affect you if you were to apologize to another but their response was the refusal to grant forgiveness?

Did you know that, whether or not someone grants you forgiveness, the most important aspect of forgiveness begins within you?

Did you know that if you forgive someone but hang onto the memories associated with the harm, then you have not honestly or wholeheartedly offered forgiveness?

If forgiveness begins within you, why then are you hanging onto the past? If you are hanging onto the past, then you have not truly forgiven yourself or another.

Steps Towards Achieving Forgiveness

1.) Acknowledge and take responsibility for your actions.

2.) Accept the ramifications of your actions.

3.) Repent for the wrongs you have committed.

4.) Forgive yourself and, if applicable, ask the forgiveness of others.

5.) Accept the forgiveness.

6.) Leave the past behind you, understanding that your wrongs are a part of your history but have nothing to do with your identity or your destiny.

Relax and Meditate Daily	Journal Your Inner Thoughts	Practice Focused Breathing

CHAPTER THIRTEEN

GRATEFULNESS

Gratitude is the fairest blossom which springs from the soul.

—Henry Ward Beecher

Have you ever noticed that when you are grateful, the bad seems to take a back seat in your life? Have you ever been around someone who was ungrateful? What was it like to be around that person? How did you react or feel? What was the experience like for you? Are you grateful for your life? Have you ever experienced a moment of ungratefulness?

When we express gratefulness to be alive, the issues in our lives become challenges and our lives becomes an Olympic event waiting for us to compete. Have you ever watched an Olympic event? What makes the minds of Olympic athletes strive for their very best? How are their minds different from your own? Are they? Do you feel that you have a similar mindset? Or is your mindset bleak, discouraged, overwhelmed, and overworked?

Olympians are not unlike you and me. They, too, have had to struggle, develop, and engage in this life. Olympians have had to attend school and learn the basic human concepts of survival. However, there seems to be a vast difference between the mindset of an Olympian and that of the common person. What is it? What allows for some individuals to literally strive for gold, while others sit at the sidelines admiring their talents, fortitude, and personal drive? Have you ever wished that you had the stamina of an athlete, that ability to sustain the most rigid of physical and mental exercises? What if I told you that you have an ability to prove your very best? Would you doubt me? Would you make excuses for your ineptitude?

Your mind is no different than the Olympians'. You, too, have an ability to push yourself beyond what you have expected or others might expect. You may even present an excuse that says, "I have a physical, psychological, psychiatric, or neurological disability." Consider for a moment that you lost the use of your arms or legs, and science has shown no rationale behind your physical condition. How would this affect you? Would you allow this to slow you down? Would you simply give up? How would you see yourself? Would you see yourself in a negative context? Would life feel bleak and without hope? Would you isolate yourself from the rest of humanity? Let's look at this issue in a different perspective. What if this issue was cast on someone else? How would you relate to that person? Would you feel at odds with that person? Would you see that person as less than you or an oddity of nature? Why? What makes that person's life less than your own? What makes that person's spiritual pursuit less effective than someone who has been born with all of their physical extremities? Be honest with yourself at this moment: What occurs in your mind when you see someone with an apparent physical or mental disability? I ask that you take a moment and ponder this question in your own mind. What has crossed your mind? Have the reels in your mind ever replayed over and over again an event, a person, or situation whereby you were confronted with your own fears of the unknown? The fear that drives you from sharing life with someone who is different from you, or who conflicts with your definition of a complete person, is the same fear that drives you away from being your ultimate best.

Do you recall my story of someone slipping and falling on ice? What crosses your mind when you imagine someone slipping on ice? Are you laughing at their misfortune? Are you trying to comfort that person in the midst of their own mishap? Do you recall a television commercial that depicts a woman who presses a medical pendant to inform a monitoring service company that she has fallen and can't get up? What crosses your mind when reflecting on this particular commercial? Would your response be different if she was not frail, disabled, or of a senior age? What if she were younger than you? Would it make a difference if she fell on a patch of ice or bare floor instead of a carpet?

Life is truly an amazing experience. We have opportunities that can propel us to be greater, and losses that can teach us invaluable lessons. We can learn from all of sorts of individuals and be inspired by the greatest among us. Why then, if we are always seeking to learn, are we not seeking to be an inspiration to others? Why is it that others can have all sorts of obstacles and challenges facing them head on and their personality seems to pull them through? Can I develop the skills to become a more competitive individual? Why is it that some individuals are perceivably invincible?

How can they gird their loins knowing that they are facing life's battles? I am too tired and weak to fight the good fight of life. What will it take for me to gain the gusto to do something remarkable in my own life?

What is it that makes some go-getters and others complacent? It is rather simple; it is the unconditional belief in self. It is the unconditional love and acceptance of self. Whether I am a winner or loser in an Olympic game, I know that I love and accept myself unconditionally. It is not uncommon for an athlete who wins a race to be harder on himself or herself for not getting it 100% right: the "I could have done better" line of thought. I, too, used to be one of these individuals. I had a hard time accepting my victories and losses. It seemed that I not only had to be the victor of life's challenges, but also the victor of my mind. For many, a victory in life may seem hollow without a mental victory occurring within their own being. In fact, it is the mental victory that enhances all other victories of life.

How can I obtain the mental victory of life? It is something that has to be experienced through patience, perseverance, and persistence. Victory in your mind will not occur overnight. It is beyond becoming comfortable with yourself; it is the unconditional acceptance of self that will help you to develop into the greatest of mental athletes.

You may describe yourself as unmotivated, discouraged, and disinterested in life. For you, the fruit of life may have lost its sweetness, becoming bitter, tasteless, and sour. You may have lost the drive you once had to live life to its fullest. Life may no longer represent for you a challenge, but may have become a sort of roadblock ceasing your ability to move forward. Let me ask you: When was the last time that you asked yourself, "How can I gain victory in this life?" When was the last time that you felt a personal drive to live life to its fullest? Have you lost the taste of life's sweetness? Can you recall the flavor of life? What was it like to bite into the essence of life? Did you think, "Hey, what can I gain from this day? What can I gain from this moment?" When was the last time that you saw yourself with unconditional eyes?

If you want to truly live life to its fullest, you must begin to expect that you deserve a life beyond what you are currently experiencing. For peak performance to occur in your life, you must reach out and take hold of your life. You are more than a physical entity simply struggling to survive on this earth. You are a spirit, and that spirit desires to live life abundantly.

You have a profound greatness to be offered in this life. Why should only athletes, the elite, and the special experience the fruit of life? Arguably, although they may be achieving greatness on this planet, they may not be experiencing internal greatness within their own person. If you desire to experience internal greatness, why are you waiting to live?

Internal greatness can be achieved through patience, perseverance, and persistence. You must begin to accept yourself fully, despite your failures or your successes. You must also begin to see yourself as greater than your failures or your successes. Have you ever known someone who seemed to have it all? Did they have the right job, the right partner, the right home, the right lifestyle, the right life? Please note that having it all materially is not an indication that they have it all internally. More than likely, you have heard about a celebrity taking his or her own life. You have also probably heard about a celebrity tragically dying due to a drug overdose, an eating disorder, or some other unfortunate path they chose to pursue. It is unfortunate when you hear about a life suddenly lost because of bad choices. What occurs within the framework of your mind when you hear these types of stories? What is your instant reaction? Are you apt to feeling a penetrating regret for their loss? Do you feel a sense of emptiness, sadness, or despair because of their loss? If so, you are not unlike many others who hear about loss in this life. Loss is sad, it can prove discouraging, and it can prove heartbreaking. Why, then, aren't you ensuring that your life is lived abundantly? Why, then, aren't you practicing skills that boost your confidence, pure confidence; quench those negative thoughts of self-doubt; and align yourself with skills to enhance your overall quality of life? What are you waiting for? Are you waiting for that day that you retire? Are you waiting for the day that you strike it rich? More than likely, if you are waiting for some fateful day, that day will never come, and—sadly—your life will have never been experienced. You will never be capable of saying, "I lived life to its fullest."

Life can throw curve balls of discouragement, and we all have moments of relapse, but through daily training, your life can be lived beyond your wildest of imaginations. Your life can be enriched through daily physical and mental exercise. You can gain confidence, self-assurance, self-esteem, personal approval, and personal security through daily mental exercises. It is possible to love yourself unconditionally and without any attachments or conditions lining the walls of your life. Life can become a daily challenge rather than a consequence of being born.

For many years, I have trained my patients and others to experience life's richness. I have witnessed a transformation of many who are willing to pursue life's richness, and I, too, have grown through my personal and professional training. I have been honored to watch many conquer their fears and seek to be victors over their challenges. Are you ready to pursue life? Are you ready to live a life beyond your own past expectations? Are you ready to defeat the past, its heartaches, its trials, its tribulations? Have you decided to look at living in this present moment? If so, let's begin the process of developing your ability to live in this very moment.

CHAPTER CHALLENGE: ENCOURAGING GRATEFULNESS

When you are grateful, the negative mind is set aside. When we are grateful, we are acknowledging the good that has been granted in our lives. Gratitude is being unconditionally thankful. Gratefulness sees the good and the bad as mere experiences lived in this life. Gratefulness is the acknowledgment that our lives are the divine inspiration of a higher being. When we are grateful, we are thankful for the opportunity to live this life. If you are living a state of ungratefulness, you are telling the spiritual world that you are displeased with this opportunity to live life. As a spiritual being, you should seek to live each moment as though it might be your last. By being grateful, you are sharing in the responsibility of life and the challenge to live life abundantly. May your life be filled with a grateful attitude.

How can you express your gratefulness to be alive? The following assignment will encourage the expression of your gratefulness.

I am grateful to be alive because...

Relax and Meditate Daily	Journal Your Inner Thoughts	Practice Focused Breathing

CHAPTER FOURTEEN

LIVING IN THE MOMENT

Today is life—the only life you are sure of. Make the most of today.

—Dale Carnegie

You have probably heard many life gurus say that, to live life, you must live it in the moment. What does that ultimately mean? Are we not all living a life? You can live in this physical life and be decaying in your mental life. In recent years, researchers have begun looking at the correlation of the mind, body, and spirit. Furthermore, they have begun researching how negative attitudes, stress, anxiety, fear, and other negative thought patterns can impact not only your overall attitude and perception of life, but can physically alter your neurological, biological, and physiological ability to function properly. *In fact, it has been discovered that weight gain and weight loss can be altered depending on your overall perception of life.*

The keys to living life are endurance, confidence, assurance, security, self-worth, self-esteem, unconditional approval, unconditional attraction, unconditional love, and unconditional acceptance of yourself. As a therapist, I have heard many times that when someone doubts their ability to perform in a role in life, they are rarely capable of performing at their peak performance. Why is this? It boils down to the following: If I cannot fully love and accept myself, then I am placing limits on my ability to live life abundantly. If I hold a mirror of disapproval up to myself, then I doubt my ability to perform my role in life. If I lose my attraction of self, then I will doubt my internal and external being. Therefore, I am no longer capable of feeling worthy of others, because I no longer see myself as unconditional.

What does it mean to be unconditional? If you have an unconditional mindset, then you see yourself beyond your failures or successes. You wholeheartedly and unequivocally accept your spirit and your person as being worthy and lovable.

Achieving an unconditional state of mind occurs when you are capable of seeing yourself beyond your body. In recent years, I have heard many theorists discuss the concept of creating or becoming mentally tough. In fact, the complete opposite is necessary to live a fulfilled life. Arguably, we train our soldiers, paramilitary, and other combative professionals to girt their loins with physical toughness, but the truth of their mental toughness is frequently exposed when they have psychological breaks. In recent years, we have witnessed the decay of mental readiness, which is often overshadowed by the physical readiness of our young military men and women. It is gut-wrenching to watch as men and women who have given their lives to serve our countries lose hope and choose to commit a variety of atrocities on the people that they serve. If the achievement of physical soundness was enough, then those who are serving as soldiers or any other paramilitary force should be of the soundest of minds. However, the truth is that psychological preparedness is overshadowed by the need for physical preparedness. It is therefore prudent that if you desire to live a life and to live abundantly, you must refine your way of thinking. If you truly desire a life of complete acceptance then you—yes, you—must begin physically, mentally, and spiritually exercising your entire being. Life is about living, so why are you waiting to experience this life?

CHAPTER CHALLENGE: THE LOST ART OF JOURNALING

As we have become a technological society, we have lost our ability to communicate through the art of writing. The art of writing inspires imagination, inspiration, and communication, and enhances our ability to critically think. Likewise, it is physical exercise such as journaling that stimulates our brain, allowing it to operate at its maximum capacity. In this exercise, you will journal your thoughts on the concept of *living in the moment*. Are you living in the moment? Have you ever chosen to reside in the past?

Journaling is an incredible exercise that stimulates your mind, your body, and your spirit. It is an exercise that can unite your spirit with the spiritual world. It is an excellent source for expressing yourself, clarifying your ambitions, and solving difficult problems. Journaling uses both hemispheres of the brain, which ultimately means that you are exercising your complete physical mind. The exercise of journaling can help with fears, temptations, uncertainties and confusion. Furthermore, journaling is beneficial for increasing one's awareness, self-esteem, self-worth and personal insights. Finally, journaling is the most beneficial when you are willing to be authentically you.

Today's date: _____

Journal title: _____

Relax and Meditate Daily	Journal Your Inner Thoughts	Practice Focused Breathing

CHAPTER FIFTEEN

THE UNCONDITIONAL STATE

> Love is a force that connects us to every strand of the
> universe, an unconditional state that characterizes human
> nature, a form of knowledge that is always there for us if
> only we can open ourselves to it.
>
> —Emily Hilburn Sell

As very young children, we are unconditionally accepting of our parents,
guardians, and authorities. As we age, our minds are filled with negative
information, situations, and events that alter our unconditional state.
Although the unconditional state remains a part of our spiritual being,
our physical being departs from this truth. What does it mean to be
unconditional? What is an unconditional state? The power of the
unconditional mind comes directly from our spiritual being. In principle,
being unconditional infers a fundamental truth that says *No matter how I
look, think, or perform, I am worthy, I am acceptable, I am attractive, I am
loved.* When we utilize our conditional minds, we have a foundation of
lies that tells us we are no longer worthy, no longer acceptable, no longer
attractive, and ultimately unloved or unlovable.

As a parent, I have learned the true meaning of unconditional love. The
unconditional mind informs us that there are no limits to our ability
to love or forgive. The unconditional mind sees us as always attractive,
acceptable, and worthy. Why, then, are we plagued with the conditional
state of thought? As humans, we frequently confuse the unconditional
form of love with other forms of love. The Greeks described three primary
forms of love: *eros,* the physical or sexual form of love; *philia,* the brotherly
or friendship form of love; and *agape,* the unconditional form of love, also
referred to as a spiritual or parental form of love. Agape teaches us that
we can love despite someone's wrongs or rights. Furthermore, it informs
us that there are no deeds good or bad that will cause another to lose favor
in our eyes. Have you ever encountered someone that you loved despite
their negative actions? If so, you have been capable of separating the person
from their deeds, thus you have already practiced the unconditional state

of being. Have you ever been loved in spite of your own negative actions? Have you ever felt like you really don't deserve someone's love? If so, you have received an unconditional state of acceptance and love.

Is there someone in your life that you would accept no matter what? Who is that person? Why are they capable of receiving your unconditional acceptance but others are not? What about yourself, your own person, can you always accept yourself unconditionally? What criteria have you placed on yourself that says, "I can only accept and love myself if"? Are you placing these same conditions on others? If you have placed them on your own life, you can be assured that you have placed them on the lives of others. If we have not experienced an unconditional love for ourselves and in ourselves, we will be incapable of sharing such a love until we know it internally. Unconditional love teaches us to unconditionally accept, approve of, be attracted to, be secure in, be assured of, and be confident in ourselves. If we cannot unconditionally accept our own person, then how can we unconditionally accept the life of another? The unconditional state of being begins the process of health and happiness. The unconditional state informs us that no matter what actions, beliefs, mistakes, or heartaches occur in our lives, we will always accept our being.

For many, the unconditional makes no sense, because they know not their internal being. I am not speaking of a religious being but rather the spiritual being that we are and that dwells within us. Have you ever attended a funeral? Have you ever walked up to a person who has died and looked them in the face? Did you touch their hands or face? What was it like for you? What went through your mind while you were in this person's presence? For most people, they describe such experiences as cold or indifferent. I have heard numerous times that when someone encountered a lifeless body, they could not feel the presence of the person. What is ultimately being said when we describe a body as cold, empty, or indifferent? We are describing the absence of the spirit from the body. Remember that the human body is simply a shell of our existence, for when we die, our physical bodies decay and our spiritual bodies vacate.

The human body is a container of our internal being. It is separate from our spiritual being. The human body is simply a cargo container carrying our spiritual nature to our next destination. Moreover, the human body does not represent its spiritual cargo, just as a cargo container does not represent the merchandise within it. Although we look at the human body and contemplate the beauty of the external, the internal being—the spirit within us—is the greatest of all.

Why do we struggle with the unconditional state? We struggle with the unconditional state because we see the outer person as a representation of the internal being. We think that an external act represents the true nature of the person. If we can get beyond seeing people as their external bodies, we could begin truly accepting and loving others despite their external errors. I am not saying that there are not consequences for our external behaviors. What I am saying is that who we are externally is bound to make mistakes because it is not of a pure and spiritual nature. Therefore, if we make a mistake externally—whether it is an error in judgment, perception, or thought—we owe it to ourselves to forgive our external selves. Likewise, it is important to remember that our physical minds are separate thinkers from our spiritual minds. It is possible to control our physical minds, but we need to be in tune with our spiritual being before we can alter our physical bodies or minds.

If we desire to unconditionally love and accept others, we must be accepting of our own person with the same unconditional love and acceptance. We must take away the parameters of conditions that disallow us from fully experiencing such an unconditional state of being. If we are living in an unconditional state, we feel worthy, attractive, acceptable, and loving, and have no reason not to approve of our spiritual being. Our society has become so plagued with finding fault lines in the lives of others that we have television shows dedicated to searching for our mistakes. In fact, we have television shows like TMZ, the sole purpose of which is to diminish the character of others, mocking them like it is some sort of childhood game. We have lost our sensibility and our love for our fellow human. As a society, we thrive on hearing and gossiping about the fallen, rarely speaking of others' good deeds and acts.

Why is it that we thrive on the negative rather than positive? Why can we not fully and unconditionally accept and love our fellow human? It stems from our own depravity. We have become immoral, corrupted, and wicked because we seek to dominate our fellow human. We have forgotten what it means to be a village, a community, and a people of the same race. We no longer voyage across seas to discover new lands, new goods, new lives; rather we are now seeking to take over the world like a bunch of pirates seeking to seize command of a ship. We seek to destroy the lives of others and find pleasure in hearing about our fellow humans' mistakes. How, you may ask, can I become an individual filled with an unconditional mind? The change begins within you. First of all, you must desire to change your being. Secondly, you must be proactive in your life by identifying the need to be in harmony within your mind, body, and spirit. If you choose only to focus on one of these in your life, your life will become imbalanced, and the overall good will be lost.

Unconditional love reaches its greatness when we experience it firsthand. It can move mountains, change lives, and prevent decay of the human spirit. The unconditional experience seeks to promote the individual.

CHAPTER CHALLENGE: PERSONAL LOVE LETTER

When was the last time that you expressed an unconditional love for yourself? Do you find it difficult expressing love for yourself? This is not a prideful sort of love but an agape love, the type of love that should dwell deep within your spirit. You should not avoid, hesitate, or reserve affectionate words you may have for yourself. Allow your words to be sincere, complete, and without reservation. You wholeheartedly and unconditionally love yourself because _____. Be certain that you are writing this letter for yourself. Do not reserve your thoughts or it will be without merit. You may want to review this letter in the future. You may also want to make a regular habit of writing yourself a personal love letter.

Today's date: _____

Love letter title: _____

Relax and Meditate Daily	Journal Your Inner Thoughts	Practice Focused Breathing

CHAPTER SIXTEEN

CREATING AN UNCONDITIONAL STATE

> I believe that the struggle against death, the unconditional
> and self-willed determination to live, is the mode of power
> behind the lives and activities of all outstanding men.

—Hermann Hesse

When I seek to create an unconditional state within my being, I begin to realize that my identity has nothing to do with my rights or wrongs. It has nothing to do with my past, present, or future. My identity is that I am a spirit, and my spirit desires to thrive on this planet. As a spirit, I am a person who resides in an unconditional state of always loving, trusting, accepting, believing, and approving of my person. Likewise, in the unconditional state, I will always be attracted to myself, confident in myself, worthy of myself, assured in myself, and safe with myself.

In an unconditional state, there is nothing to fear. What is fear? Fear is an emotional response to a known or perceived threat. Should we fear? Absolutely not, because if we are in an unconditional state, then there is nothing to fear. If I am good with myself, loving of myself, then when bad occurs, I see it as a challenge. A challenge is something to overcome. It is not a barrier blocking our ability to survive. If I am a spirit, then I realize that this challenge is simply a stepping stone in my life's journey. If I am good with myself, then I am good with others, so I know that my life has served a positive purpose. Fear tells us that we are weak, vulnerable, incomplete. We are not. Although I may not contain within my physical body the same strength as another, my spiritual body is equal to all.

Fear is the greatest obstacle. Fear ceases our ability to fully function. Fear accepts false messages as truth, turning the truth of life into a false message. It is fear that causes a singer to be incapable of performing on stage. It is fear that causes the athlete to question his or her own choices. It is fear that limits us. It is fear that drives us away from the potential of human greatness.

We are all displaced by fear. Fear seeks to take over our lives. It tells us that we are inept and incapable of competing with others. It is fear that lures us away from asking someone out on a date. Fear stifles our ability to breathe and can stop our heart from functioning. The scientific community has confused fear with awareness. Awareness draws our attention to possible threats, whereas fear makes us feel vulnerable to the threat. If I am a spirit, then what do I have to fear? The majority of the world's religions teach of a life beyond this one here on earth. If I firmly believe that there is a life beyond the now, then what do I have to fear? If I am threatened and if my life is taken, won't I be going to the Great Beyond? Therefore, what can cause me to fear?

No human, machine, or being on this earth or beyond can cause me to fear. Fear is a stimulus, an emotional response to a perceived threat or the possibility of threat, but it should be fear that has no room in our lives. As spiritual beings, we know that this life is not the end of the road. We know that this life is a part of the spiritual journey.

When I was young, I feared. I feared a great deal of this life. I feared planes plummeting to the earth; I feared falling off of the side of a building; I feared what others thought of me and what they could possibly be thinking of me; I even feared my spirit. I feared the absence of friends, a lack of friends, the passing of friends; I feared my performance in this life; I feared failure, embracing it as though it offered me comfort. I feared, I feared—I feared myself, others, and the essence of life. My fears had no validity, no relevance, no place in my life. Fear caused me to doubt my ability as a student, as a performer, as a person. I have been taught that fear is an emotional response of my body and my physical mind, but if I have the assurance of my spirit, how can I have any form of fear in this life? If I know that my spirit guides me, then how can I fear externally? Fear should have no place in my life. As I aged and as I matured as a spirit, I began to recognize how fear had consumed my life. I began learning how many of my choices in life had occurred because of fear. Likewise, I began to learn that a life without fear is truly limitless. Isn't it discouraging to watch a commercial promoting the newest antianxiety medication? What would your life look like if you were no longer dependent on a medication but rather dependent on the knowledge of your spirit?

Life should be lived with confidence, assurance, and security. If I am living life in a timid way, even for a moment, I am losing out on that moment of life. If I show timidity, I am much like a helpless animal cowering, frightened, and fearful of a situational outcome. If I know that I am a spirit, even if I know that my physical life may end, I should find comfort in knowing that my life will continue beyond the physical body.

Although the fear of failure is not the only fear, it is one of the greatest common fears amongst humans. In fact, did you know that the fear of failure is ranked highest amongst all fears? Have you ever feared failing at something? Have you ever feared disappointing yourself or another, so you simply didn't try? Why? Did you realize that if you fear failure, you are also fearing the loss of approval, acceptance, attraction, and love? If you fear failure, you lack confidence, assurance, security, and knowledge of your self-worth, and ultimately lose your identity. Isn't it something that the fear of failure and fear itself break down the ability to see ourselves as unconditional spiritual beings? Fear destroys our ability to unconditionally love, respect, and accept ourselves. If I fear failing, then I have set conditions on my life. If I fear failing, I may choose not to try, therefore essentially failing because I never put forth the effort. What is wrong with failing? Failing expresses to us that we have room for improvement. The fear of failure expresses to us that we might as well not try.

Conquering fear returns us to the unconditional state. If I am unconditionally accepting of myself and I fail, I see it as a challenge rather than as an identity marker. You must remember that whatever mistakes you make in this life as well as whatever successes you have in this life are not a representation of who you are, for you are a spirit and not a failure.

Many religions teach us that fear is not of God or of our spiritual nature. Fear is not intended for our lives. "For God has not given you a spirit of fear, but of power and of love and of a sound mind." (2 Timothy 1:7) If you are living a life of fear, then you are not living life; rather, you have taken on a survival role.

Regardless of what you have been told, or what you have told yourself, what would this life look like if you could not fail? Have you ever had a moment in your life when you felt that you were invincible? Have you ever felt like you could not fail? What was it like? How did you respond to it? Fear stifles our ability to be productive. It places roadblocks and detours us from our dreams. Fear is not a friend but rather a decisive enemy of our lives.

Overcoming fear takes confidence, assurance, security, approval, acceptance, and personal attraction. It can only occur if we are in an unconditional state. The conditional state tells us that if we cannot make the mark, then we are a failure. Overcoming fear only occurs when we train our minds, with help from our spirit, to see ourselves in an unconditional light. It takes practice, practice, practice to begin recognizing when we are making mistakes or errors in our judgment. The power of conquering fear will occur once you begin to

1.) Recognize the role that fear has had in your life
2.) Change your perception of self as well as your attitudes that are based on that perception
3.) Recognize that your thoughts and mindset can prove negative obstacles
4.) Train your mind to think, speak, and respond positively
5.) Begin recognizing that who you are is not a representation of your physical state but rather is a spiritual being waiting to be unleashed

Despite what life has dealt you, you must begin to see these obstacles as mere challenges. Do you enjoy a challenge? Have you ever ran a race, played an instrument, or competed in a chess tournament? Has life ever presented you with a complex puzzle that you had to figure out? If so, then you have been faced with a challenge. Let me take this one step further: Have you been driving and suddenly found yourself stuck in mud or snow? Have you ever ran out of gas? Have you ever arrived home thinking about having a tall glass of milk only to find that your milk has soured? If so, then you, too, have been faced with a challenge. Challenges do not have to be major events. In fact, most challenges that we face on a daily basis are minor. Nevertheless, what occurs in your mind when these negative challenges are presented is most likely what will occur when the positive ones are presented. Therefore, you must challenge your overall way of thinking. Whether you are challenged with a major or minor event, you must begin to see them as mere challenges. Personally, I now like a challenge and will occasionally look forward to them. They are like barbells in my cognitive weight room. How do you respond to challenges?

Challenges are simply a way of life presenting growth. Growth encourages you to take responsibility for things you have control over and accept the things that are out of your control.

As a reminder, let's review the unconditional and conditional states of mind. An unconditional state helps you to rid yourself of the conditions that bog you down. The conditional state increases your fears and insecurities. The conditional state uses negativity to alter your mindset from positivity. This alteration causes you to feel vulnerable, insecure, defensive, obsessive, regretful, and reactive. The conditional state uses your fears to detour you from being your best. It uses blame and shame to discourage you from feeling your best. The unconditional state emphasizes you, your spiritual nature. The unconditional state recognizes that you are a person of worth, value, approval, attraction, and love. The unconditional state helps you to unequivocally accept and love yourself. Therefore, once we know and recognize our right to live in an unconditional state, we are freed from our fears, shame, and blame and the rest of life's negative roadblocks.

The conditional state makes you feel vulnerable. Have you ever felt vulnerable? Have you ever feared for your life or the life of someone else? Are you a reactive person? We seldom see being reactive as a good thing, but our reactions are based on our responses. If we have a positive mindset, then our reactions should be positive. If we have a negative mindset, then our conditional response and reaction will be negative.

CHAPTER CHALLENGE: REVIEWING OUR FEARS

When was the last time you felt frightened? What was it that caused you to fear? Can you describe the fear? Was it mind-numbing or life-altering? Were you changed by your fear? How profound of an effect did the fearful event or situation have on your life?

Fear can be stifling. It can make it difficult for you to breathe properly. You may react emotionally and subconsciously. Fear may prevent you from living life fully and completely. It may constrain you from being yourself, forcing you to alter your entire person. Fear has no place in your life. Fear cannot threaten you or make you feel embarrassed. Fear can only have an effect if you allow it the right and the privilege to reside in you.

You may have been challenged by fear. You may even have been challenged by a variety of fears. Today is the day to begin overcoming them and learn to be the master of your life. Today is the day to gain ground over your fears. The following are a set of questions. Do not think about your answers. Do not fret over your answers. Simply respond to each question with sincerity, honesty, and wholeness of heart. Do not be afraid. You are not going to be judged, criticized, or questioned about your answers. The answers are solely for your own personal growth and development. May this exercise begin you on a journey of hope, prosperity, and happiness.

1.) My fears are alleviated when…?

2.) My greatest fear is…?

3.) I feel safest when…?

4.) My fears increase when I am with…?

5.) My fears cause me to have panic attacks. □ True   □ False

6.) I am aware of my fears, but I am without coping strategies to deal with my fears. □ True   □ False

7.) I drink caffeine, smoke cigarettes, or consume sugar on a regular basis. □ True   □ False

Did you know that smoking, caffeine, and sugar can heighten your anxiety and stress levels?

If you are finding that you are experiencing elevations of stress, anxiety, or panic, you might consider eliminating some or all of these substances from your diet.

8.) Were you engaging in a negative conversation before feeling fearful? If so, express how this conversation elevated your state of fear, anxiety, or stress.

9.) Were you feeling exhausted, tired, or simply lethargic before the onset of your fears? *If so, be certain that you are receiving plenty of rest and relaxation.*

10.) Are your dreams filled with fearful issues, reminders, or events? *If so, you may consider receiving psychological counseling to help deal with your past. Remember, our past has no bearing on our present.*

11.) When I am fearful, my mind is filled with the following false statements:

12.) When I am fearful, my heart rate increases; my palms become sweaty; my breathing is rapid; I have sensations of dizziness, fogginess, or absence of thoughts; and/or I experience an upset stomach, indigestion, or gastrointestinal difficulties? ☐ True   ☐ False

Alleviating Our Fears

1.) Perform breathing exercises as follows:

> a.) Lie flat on your back. Be certain that all noises, sounds, and distractions are set aside. Clear all obstacles away so that you are comfortable. Place your hands to your side. Gently close your eyes. Slowly take a breath inward, then slowly exhale it. Begin to focus your mind on the process of inhaling and exhaling. You may wish to count to 5. If so, slowly count to 5 as you take a breath inward, hold it, then exhale it. You may wish to repeat this until you feel calm and relaxed, clearing your mind of all unwanted feelings, thoughts, and emotions.

> b.) If you are unable to lie down or are in a place or situation in which there are no beds, recliners, or couches, find and sit in a stable and comfortable chair. Sit straight

up and with your feet flat and on the ground. Cross your hands but do not clench them. Be certain that you are sitting straight up with your feet flat and on the ground, and your hands crossed. At this point, take a breath inward, then exhale it. Be certain that your eyes are gently closed. You may wish to count to 5. If so, slowly count to 5 as you take a breath inward, hold it, then exhale it. You may wish to repeat this until you feel calm and relaxed, clearing your mind of all unwanted feelings, thoughts, and emotions.

Repeat this exercise as many times as needed. Remember, you may desire to begin counting slowly to five, holding it, then releasing it. You may also use a metronome to help you keep focused on the counting rhythm.

2.) Consider taking a long slow walk. Wherever you live, get yourself somewhere that you can look at nature. Whether you reside in a city or in the country, consider finding a park and simply relaxing. If there are children playing, listen to their laughter. Savor the moment, breathe deeply and slowly.

3.) Use positive self-talk and self-reflection to help eliminate your fears, anxieties, and stressors. Remind yourself that you are safe. You may desire to repeat positive statements. You may desire to say such statements as

   a) "I am safe, secure, and unharmed."
   b) "I am experiencing fear based on my emotional state. My anxiety, stress, and fear have no bearing on my reality."
   c) "I have control over my mind, body, and spirit."
   d) "I am deserving of calmness and serenity."
   e) "My fears have no place in my life."
   f) "I do not have to invite my fears inward; they have no right in my life."

In addition, you may desire to compose your own positive statements:

4.) Have someone that you are comfortable with rub your neck, head, and shoulders.

5.) Treat yourself to a cup of decaffeinated tea, a warm bath, and lit candles.

6.) Engage in pleasant conversation.

7.) Consider reading a humorous book, comic strip, or magazine.

8.) Chew a piece of gum, focusing your thoughts on the number of times you chew.

9.) Provide yourself with a distraction. This is a great alleviator of fears, anxieties, stressors, and even anger. If you are experiencing any negative emotion or feelings, consider implementing the following to alleviate these negative conditions:

> a.) Consider physical exercise. Did you know that physical exercise can help regulate your endorphins and calm the adrenaline experienced during a fight-or-flight event? Exercise. Even the simple task of walking swiftly can alleviate your heightened state of fear.
>
> b.) Take a cold shower.
>
> c.) Find a song on the radio and sing with your whole heart.
>
> d.) Count the trees in a field or the number of veins on a leaf. For an even greater challenge, consider reaching for a handful of sand, then counting each grain separately.

10.) Write an affectionate letter to yourself or someone else.

11.) Chop, stack, or toss wood.

12.) Consider intimacy as an option to alleviate your state of fearfulness, stressfulness, or anxiety.

13.) Do deep abdominal breathing.

14.) Consider taking yourself for your own version of a Happy Meal. Enjoy and savor the meal, clearing the negative thoughts that are plaguing your mind.

Be aware of your mind, body and spiritual conditions. Exercise your mind, body, and spirit on a regular basis. If you are finding it difficult to manage your mind, body, or spirit, consider seeking the advice of a practitioner to help guide and teach you to manage your overall person.

Relax and Meditate Daily	Journal Your Inner Thoughts	Practice Focused Breathing

CHAPTER SEVENTEEN

BEING OFFENDED

> When you are offended at any man's fault, turn to yourself and study your own failings. Then you will forget your anger.
>
> —Epictetus

All too often, people are offended. Being offended means that you are feeling upset, annoyed, or perhaps resentful because of a particular situation. If you are offended, you are displeased with someone else's behaviors. Why be offended? If I am offended, then I am saying to you that you owe me. You owe me respect, dignity, or acceptance. See? It returns us back to our own being. If I can approve of myself, am confident in myself, secure in myself, assured of myself, worthy of myself, and attracted to myself, then I ultimately unconditionally love myself. Therefore, if I am offended, I am looking to you for approval. You might be saying, "Now, wait a second—I am not seeking someone out who offends me." Actually, you are. You may not be saying that you want him or her to like you, but you are saying that you want him or her to respect you.

What is respect? There are two types of respect. The first type of respect occurs in the human body. The second type of respect involves the spiritual context of our being. The first type of respect is a feeling of great importance in our society. Have you ever heard someone say, "You need to respect your elders"? Why should I show acceptance or approval of someone that I virtually don't know? Why should I respect someone for being my elder? Why should I respect someone for having more education or knowledge than I have? Why should I respect you as a human? Human respect has nothing to do with the second type of spiritual respect. Spiritual respect sees every person as a spiritual brother or sister. Spiritual respect makes everyone equal, whereas human respect tells us that we are not equal. Human respect can be, and is often, demanded. We are told and taught to respect authority, our teachers, our religious leaders, our elders, our politicians, our parents and siblings, our aunts and uncles, and our grandparents. We are taught that respect is a value. If I respect you, then I value your place in my life.

I ask you, why should I respect you? The human you? What have you done to gain my respect? What have I done to lose others' respect? Human respect and spiritual respect are not synonymous. Human respect involves solely the outer person, its behaviors, its choices, its decisions, its life. Spiritual respect sees everyone and everything as a spiritual being. It recognizes that all life is spiritual. It sees the spiritual context of life as the most important. As a human species, we do not respect one another. We may think we respect one another, but when was the last time you helped a homeless person, a person of need, an enemy? Do you sincerely respect your entire community of humans? What if a neighbor stopped by your door with conflicting religious beliefs? Would you or could respect this person? Or are you selective with your respect?

We frequently confuse human respect with our spiritual need for respect. If we were to spiritually respect every being on this planet, there would be no wars, disputes, or disagreements. You have heard of respect for human life. I say we take it one step further. We should have respect for the spiritual side of life, which in turn causes us to respect all humans. Human respect only allows respect for those with similar mind sets; spiritual respect goes well beyond the human mind, accepting all of humanity as spirit.

Our human quest is to survive; our spiritual quest is to unite.

CHAPTER CHALLENGE: WORKING TOWARDS
INCREASING AWARENESS

Why have you chosen to be offended? When we are offended, we are essentially seeking to be wronged. Allowing yourself to take offense to something seldom leads to productive outcomes. When we are offended, we are hurt by another's actions, deeds, or communication. Have you ever been offended by another's actions, deeds, or communication? How you ever felt as though someone had wronged you? If so, you have been offended or taken offense. Have you ever offended someone else? What was the offense? Being offended blocks the pathway of change. Feeling offended essentially says, "I am hurt by your lack of respect for me." Why are you seeking to gain another's person respect in the first place? If you unconditionally respect yourself, then you will respect others.

Stopping the Offense Caboose

Why allow yourself to take offense to others actions, deeds, or communication? Will you follow the thoughts of others? If you are truly in charge of your own thoughts, deeds, and actions, then you have no time to dwell on another's thoughts, deeds, or actions. Being offended says, "You owe me," "You've wronged me," "You've deeply wounded me."

Describe the last time that you made a conscious choice to be offended.

Why were you offended?

Did you feel that someone trampled on your rights to be respected?

When I am offended, I am essentially saying, "I am seeking your acceptance, approval or respect."

Have you ever been offended by the use of

    a)   Cursing in public?
    b)   Sexual innuendoes?
    c)   Distasteful jokes, humor, or stories?
    d)   Off-the-cuff remarks?

e)   *Wrong* conversations?
    i.) Conversations about religion or politics
    ii.) Racially or sexually discriminatory conversations
f)   When someone disagrees with your thoughts, impressions, or belief systems

The behaviors, attitudes, and perceptions of others are just that; they are uniquely theirs. If you take offense to another's deeds, actions, or communication, you are essentially saying that they have to agree with you.

If you are struggling with these issues, then you may need to overcome the need to be right, heard, valued, respected, accepted, and appreciated.

If I choose to be offended, then I choose to allow harm to invade my body. If I choose to be offended, then I choose to be crippled by the deeds, actions, or communication of another. Have you ever heard the childhood rhyme, *Sticks and stones may break my bones, but words will never hurt me?* When we allow words to hurt us, we empower the words to have complete control over us. How can words hurt us? You allow them the right to label you, to define you, to try you. You are neither the good nor bad that others have experienced. You are neither your victories nor your losses; you are neither your successes nor your failures. You are a spirit, and that spirit dwells inside of you.

Society, however, has ingrained into our heads that we are what people think. They have taught us to believe that we are our failures and our successes. The truth be known, though, that when we die, when our bodies ceases to operate, we will go onward to a more magnificent world, a spiritual world filled with the unconditional. I am not my rights or wrongs. You are not your rights or wrongs. If I can see you as the spiritual being that dwells inside of you, then I can see you beyond the rights and wrongs of this life.

Let me invite you to set aside your rights and wrongs, your successes and failures, your bad deeds and good deeds. Let me invite you to experience a life of liberation, separation, and equalization.

In our world, we have created a global community that dwells on one another's past harms, intentional and unintentional. We carry around the wrongs of others as merit badges. We display these badges in a way that says, "I have a right to be angry." Did you know that if you carry the anger, stress, and anxieties associated with past wrongs, then you are carrying around a virtual ton of harm that affects your physical body? Did you know that the scientific community has shown that if you carry around these wrongs, it will affect your psychological and physiological conditions? Why would you choose to harm your body? "Well, I have a right to be angry because he hurt my feelings," you say. Forgiveness is the greatest transformer known to humankind. Forgiveness is the healer of our wrongs, and the wrongs that have been set against us. Forgiveness is the liberator of these wrongs, a separator of our minds from these past events. It brings equality to all of humanity. I am not better than you, and you are not better than me. We are both spiritual beings dwelling inside of a physical capsule. We are only on this earth for a brief moment, a twinkling of an eye.

Several years ago, I heard of two brothers who had stopped communicating. The brothers had shared their lives together. They were raised in a family that thrived on family outings, gatherings, reunions, and holidays. On one momentous occasion, the two brothers had gotten together for a family reunion. In this book, I'll disguise the brothers' names, calling the older brother Fred and the younger brother Charlie. Charlie had made a journey from far away for this particular occasion. His older brother Fred had insisted that Charlie stay at his home for the reunion. Charlie had agreed, but at the last moment, Charlie's sister Bobbi had requested that he stay with her instead. Charlie agreed to make the change, but had forgotten to inform his brother Fred. Fred was mad that his brother not only had changed his mind, but also that he had prepared to host Charlie in his home for nothing. You can imagine that the two brothers had limited conversations throughout the family reunion. Fred was so frustrated, angry, and offended that he swore he would never invite Charlie to stay with him again. Charlie was flabbergasted by Fred's hostility. He soon became angry because of Fred's outrageous claims, accusations, and anger. The two men went as far as avoiding one another and halting their communications altogether.

One day, a few years into the future, Fred was at home with his wife and children when they received a phone call from his brother Charlie. "Fred," said Charlie, "Brother, I am calling to let you know that I only have a few months left to live." "What!" exclaimed Fred, "What is happening"? Charlie proceeded to tell his brother about his battle with cancer, and how it had begun to metastasize, spreading from his stomach to his brain. Fred was filled with tears, forgetting about their long, bewildering battle of the minds and issues, exclaiming his love and requesting his forgiveness. Charlie, in a gentle spirit, informed his brother that he had long awaited a time that they could finally reunite. Charlie further expressed that he had forgotten how or why they had breached their brotherly bond. A few days later, Fred would receive another call, this time from Charlie's wife. "Fred, I am sorry to report that Charlie has lost his battle with cancer." Fred burst into tears, fell to the floor, and wept for hours over the loss of his brother. At the funeral, Fred leaned over his brother's body and said, "Brother, I may never have said it, but while I am the older of us, you were my hero."

How long are you going to carry the burdens of your past? How long will you allow your offenses to be bottled up inside of you? Will you wait like Charlie and Fred did to communicate? Or will you make amends with someone you care about? Will you stop looking to be offended? Or are you going to keep carry these offenses like some sort of merit badge?

Have you been offended by the past deeds, actions, or communications of another?

Are you going to continuing carrying these offenses around like merit badges, or are you going to put a halt to your need to be right and reconcile with another?

Are you seeking to be offended?

Do you flourish upon being right?

Do you feel a need to prove your point?

Why does it matter whether you are right or wrong?

When was the last time that you were presented with a dispute? Did you seek to be right or did you present the ultimate symbol of peace—an olive branch?

Being offended creates chaos, embittered feelings, and irrational thoughts. It is a divisive instrument created to destroy relationships and bring dysfunction. It will penetrate itself into the lives of individuals seeking to be offended. It seeks to infiltrate your mind, destroying your hope for the unconditional.

Have you been offended? Why?

With whom have you been offended?

How long have you carried the physical and psychological burden of being offended?

What can you do to bring the unconditional spirit to the lives of those you have offended? What about the lives of those who have offended you?

Do you desire to live life? Do you desire to live life abundantly?

If so, then you must stop carrying the offenses offered by others, and you must seek out your right to live life and start living it abundantly. Life is about living, and if you are delaying it, then you will never reach your life's fullest potential. May you never choose to be offended again. May you choose to live life, living it abundantly.

Relax and Meditate Daily	Journal Your Inner Thoughts	Practice Focused Breathing

CHAPTER EIGHTEEN

SPIRITUAL QUEST

> I consider myself a student of many religions. The more
> I learn, the more questions I have. For me, the spiritual
> quest will be a lifelong work in progress.
>
> —Dan Brown

On your spiritual quest, you must allow the past to be placed behind you. You must allow your mistakes and errors in life to be eliminated from your physical mind. The spiritual mind will not allow for the negative to reside, but the physical mind struggles with memories of the past. Although the spiritual mind is separate from the physical mind, it is the spiritual mind that guides your internal being. You can allow your physical mind to be in control, but if you do, you will never experience a true abundance of life. Your spiritual mind is greater than your physical mind. Your spiritual mind can protect you from harm and encourage you to become great. Your spiritual mind knows no wrongs and it keeps no records of your wrongs. Your physical mind is known to keep records of every wrong you commit. If you are living in your spiritual state, then your physical state will follow suit.

You cannot be absent from your physical mind. If this were possible, then you would no longer reside within your physical being. Therefore, it is necessary that you practice, on a daily basis, skills that can begin to unite your physical mind and body with your spiritual self.

Your quest for life should be about living, and living life to its fullest. What comes to mind when you think of living life? Do you have images of a party house, vacationing on a yacht, drinking the finest champagnes? Living life has nothing to do with partying or displaying the animalistic side of you. When you are enjoying the pleasures of life—whether they include the outdoors, the arts, or some other form of human entertainment, you are living life in the physical realm. It is important to recognize that we are physical beings, so living life abundantly physically only promotes your spiritual quest. Moreover, if your goal is to enjoy the pleasures of this life exclusively, you will segregate your spiritual being, therefore causing the spiritual side of you to be quenched. What am I saying? You cannot live life solely for the gain of the physical mind and body. Have you ever known someone that had everything that life had to offer? Were they happy on a continuum? Have you ever heard of someone taking their life, despite having it all? Why are wealthy people sad? It is because the quest in their lives has been about materials possessions, goods, and ventures. Regrettably, they never learned what real life had to offer.

A spiritual quest for life is about unconditionally accepting, loving, and approving of yourself and others. Your spiritual mind does not approve of wrongs or errors made with the physical mind; it only approves of the spiritual you. It cannot approve of the physical you. If this were so, then it would approve of the transgressions and the negative acts that we commit in this life. However, it is important to recognize that the spiritual mind accepts, loves, and approves of your spiritual you unconditionally. The spiritual you wants to unite fully with others. The spiritual you desires unity, harmony, and peace. The physical you desires to dominate, control, and discourage others from being their ultimate.

Getting to know the spiritual you is a journey. You, your spiritual self, is the being inside you that desires to live life abundantly. It desires to live life in peace. The spiritual side of you is accepting of you. Whether you're having a physically *bad hair day* or not, the spiritual you sees you as perfect, acceptable, and lovable.

Your quest, your spiritual quest, may be a long road. It may feel like an arduous road. Don't give up. Your physical mind will tell you to do so. Recall how others have fought the good fight, keeping true to their spirit. If you give in, you will never experience life and experience it abundantly.

What is life? Life is the condition with which we reside on this planet. It is a state of consciousness and activity. Life is a combination of the mind, body, and spirit. Physically, our bodies can change, our minds can adapt, and our beings will seek any means necessary to thrive. As spirits, we thrive on sharing in a common purpose, a common goal, a common unity.

We live life to its fullest when we can integrate our spiritual, mental, and physical bodies. Life is about living, so why are you delaying it? Are you waiting for the perfect day, the perfect moment, the perfect situation?

Are you waiting until you retire? Have you given up on living life? Are you merely surviving? Have you been told that this is life, so don't expect better? What is it that you are waiting for? Why are you not forcing life to be fruitful?

CHAPTER CHALLENGE: **DEVELOPING OUR**
                                        SPIRITUAL BEING

You have undoubtedly heard a variety of gurus speak, lecturers teach, and theorists propose their path to life. Developing the spiritual you is not some mystical approach to life that is only obtainable for the unique, the special, or the privileged. The approach to your spiritual path does not have to follow any particular religious teaching, doctrinal mandate, or hierarchal ranking of life. How can you experience the indwelling of your spiritual being? How can you unite your spiritual mind with your physical condition? It is through the awareness of self—the liberation of your spirit, your mind, and your body—that you will become a more complete you. You will become a more genuine and authentic person.

1.) Make a list of your positive thoughts, focusing daily on those thoughts.

2.) Spend time with yourself. Get to know the real you, the genuine you, the authentic you.

3.) Accept yourself unconditionally. Do not set conditions on yourself.

4.) Begin seeing the embodiment of your spirit in the physical you.

Once you begin loving yourself unconditionally, then you will know how to love others unconditionally.

6.) Do not avoid being alone. Your spiritual guide is seeking an opportunity to be with you.

Mindful Relaxation and Meditation

Try this exercise: Take a candle and set it in the middle of your room. Be certain to rid yourself of all outside interferences, noises, and distractions. If you have a sound machine or a water fountain, turn the machine on to play a soothing and warm sound. Make sure that you have set the sound on the lowest possible volume. Place yourself 2 to 3 feet away from the candle. Be certain that your posture is good. Do not slouch during this exercise. Sit up, straightening your spine, relax your shoulders, and begin breathing at a natural pace. Focus your attention on the candle. As you focus on the candle, you will begin noticing yourself being drawn into the candle. You will begin becoming more aware of the spiritual you.

As you get used to using candles for meditation, you may want to approach this meditative moment with an ambition or goal in mind. You may wish to meditate on a particular idea, thought, or desire. You should always be certain that your meditative goals are pure, positive, and uplifting.

There are a variety of theories, ideas, and superstitions behind using candles. Be careful that you are not drawn into any ideas that will force you into a negative place. Like our physical bodies, a candle is simply an instrument that unites you to your spirit. It is not a real representative of the spiritual world; rather, it is simply an instrument and should be looked on simply as an instrument. However, you should allow your spiritual self to help guide you when choosing the candles. It may or it may not, but be certain that the candle speaks to you, and that the candle is inviting, full of warmth, and provides you with positive vibes.

Relax and Meditate Daily	Journal Your Inner Thoughts	Practice Focused Breathing

CHAPTER NINETEEN

ACHIEVING HAPPINESS AND PEACE

Happiness is a conscious choice, not an automatic response.

—Mildred Barthel

What will it take for me to achieve happiness and peace? Pure happiness, unadulterated happiness, is peace. It is peace of mind, peace of thoughts, peace of life. You achieve this sort of peace through the unconditional love and acceptance of yourself. Pure happiness and peace are at their peak when your body is in harmony with itself. The body, the mind, and the spirit must have unity. Remember, your spirit is a part of something greater. Your spirit is a part of a deity that provides us the assurance that one day we will all live in spiritual peace and tranquility.

How can I achieve happiness on this earth? First and foremost, you must begin to recognize the roles of your body, mind, and spirit. It is important to allow these separate forms to be transformed into a newness of thought. Your spirit is your guide. Your spirit, which resides inside of your body, is a positive force that is seeking to flourish in your life. Your spiritual mind knows only the good and positive forces of life; therefore, it can help filter the negative that comes through your physical mind. Your physical mind is capable of receiving both negative and positive messages, which can sometimes become a tangled mess of information. Have you ever had or known someone who has had gum stuck in their hair? In some cases, the gum becomes so entwined and matted into the hair that it gets knotted up and tangled, and is such a mess that the only solution is cutting your hair to get rid of the gum. In our physical minds, we receive messages from all sorts of individuals. These messages can prove harmful and helpful; they can prove positive and negative. The messages' intent may be for the positive, but the human mind may misconstrue them to be negative. Although the human mind is a marvel of science, it is rather simplistic compared to the spiritual force that dwells inside of us. The spiritual serves as our guide. It serves as our protector. It serves as our life-force.

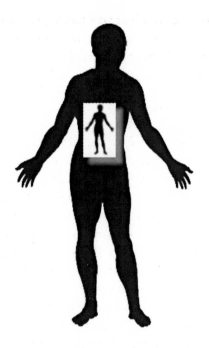

Recognizing, believing, and having faith in the spiritual mind is half the battle towards reaching your ultimate happiness. Once we believe in the spiritual indwelling, we can begin to accept and trust in its leadership and guidance. For many, the indwelling of the spiritual is difficult to believe in. They would rather think that we are made up of simple flesh, bones, and organs. It is important that you recognize, accept, trust, and believe that the spiritual exists inside of you. The spiritual is your teacher and comforter, always seeking to affirm your goodness, your attractiveness, your worth, your love, and the acceptance of you.

Happiness is a choice and a state of mind. When I feel sad or I feel happy, I have made a decision to be either sad or happy. Happiness is not giddiness or some overly inflated sense of being. Happiness is peace—the peace that knows that no matter what occurs in my life, I will be. Whether my life continues on this earth, or voyages onward, I am fully aware that my spirit will continue forth. We, as a society, often confuse happiness with momentary excitement, thrill, or some earthly pleasure. The truth is that real happiness, the genuine article of happiness, only occurs within your mind, body, and spirit. Real happiness understands that bad things happen, but allows for authentic peace to continue despite our hardships, trials, and tribulations. Many religions teach that your body is a temple of your spirit. It is true. Your body is a temple, and it contains your spirit. Therefore, why would you choose not to keep your temple holy? Why would you choose to fill your temple with negative thoughts, deeds, and actions? Your body, you mind, and your spirit are your personal trinity of life. You, the real you, have nothing to do with what people see, but it is the spirit that dwells inside of you.

Achieving happiness occurs when you allow your mind to be controlled by your spirit. It takes personal effort to achieve such happiness. Such happiness does not occur overnight, and always relies on the effort that you place inwardly and outwardly. As we grow as spiritual beings, our physical beings develop as well. The body, the mind, and the spirit begin to accept the unconditional virtues of life such as joy, peace, acceptance, attraction, assurance, confidence, and love. As our spirit, mind, and body mature, we recognize how negative versus positive information affects our beings. We begin wanting to rid our beings—physical and spiritual—of these negative thoughts, deeds, and actions. Real happiness provides you the confidence that you never thought was obtainable. Have you ever had stage fright? You may realize that it is a lack of confidence created by some internal fear centered in your human mind, but real peace eliminates that fear from your physical mind and body. Have you ever noticed that fear affects your physical mind and body? It is because we rely on our physical states for happiness, thus casting off our spiritual armor. When we are faced with even a physical battle, we should place on ourselves our spiritual armor to ward off negative thoughts.

First Lady Eleanor Roosevelt once said, "If I feel depressed, I go to work. Work is always an antidote to depression." The First Lady spoke the truth. When we work, we begin to displace all other thoughts. Therefore, negative thoughts have no room to grow. You can return to negative thoughts at another point in time, or you can decide within the internal you to rid yourself of such thoughts. If we can displace negative thoughts at work or some other venue, then why can't we do it on a continuum? I am not saying that you should run from your problems; rather, I am telling you to face your challenges and put all negative propaganda behind you. Be aware of your challenges and understand that you are the master of your life.

Real peace goes beyond explanation. Real peace reassures us in a confident and unwavering way that all situations, all events, all trials, all tribulations, all successes, and all achievements will be guided by our spirit. If we rely on the flesh, we will feel fear, but if we rely on our spirit to guide us, we will feel internal safety, security, and assurance of good things to come.

You are entitled to unconditional peace and happiness. Happiness is the ability to be authentically satisfied with the place in which you reside. It is the satisfaction of knowing that you will be provided for as a spiritual being. There are no earthly possessions, relationships, or friendships that can replace this form of happiness. A lack of happiness is simply the lack of communion, interaction, and communication within your mind, body, and spirit. If you feel an emptiness, then you have a void within your spiritual being.

When was the last time you prayed or meditated? If it has been a while, then you may need to spend some quality time reengaging your spiritual self. Happiness is the satisfaction of knowing that your life has meaning. You have not been placed on this earth as a pawn to be maneuvered to the end of a chess board, only to be replaced by a higher-ranking piece. Whether you hold a higher rank or lower rank as a physical being, your spiritual being is equal to all others. As spiritual beings, we are all entitled to peace—the real and genuine form of happiness. On earth, there are a variety of forms of happiness, but in our spirit there is only one form—the form that represents the truly unconditional form of happiness.

Achieving happiness can be accomplished through flow. Flow is the act of concentrating so intensely that no matter what occurs, your focus will be unaffected by outer forces. When you are in focus, life is clearer and sharper, and your perception is well defined. With the clarity of your focus, your spirit is unified. It is through your focus that flow occurs. Flow is the ability to move along life's streams steadily and gracefully. Flow is the ability to be so focused that all of life's obstacles seemingly and smoothly pass you by. Have you ever been so wrapped up in and focused on a specific task that you lost track of time? If so, you have experienced a moment of flow. Flow is the ability to forget your surroundings. Have you ever noticed that when you are genuinely in the moment that life seems to pass you by? This, too, is an experience of flow. When you are capable of laying aside the world's worries, frets, concerns, heartaches, and problems, then you are in a moment of flow. Why is flow important? It is vitally important, because when you are in a moment of flow, you have transferred your perceptions from this world onto the spiritual world.

You are no longer fearing the unknown. When you have lost yourself in a task, you have literally transformed yourself into a person that is living in the present.

How can I achieve happiness through the experience of flow? It can be achieved through the life you lead. Life is about living daily—living beyond fear, stress, anxiety, and the negativity of this life. It is the experience of *Hakuna matata*, a Swahili phrase meaning *There are no worries*. Flow is placing yourself unconditionally into the guidance of your spirit. Flow is important because it transports you from this life to the spiritual life.

CHAPTER CHALLENGE: **EXPERIENCING HAPPINESS THROUGH FLOW**

When was the last time you were caught up in the moment?

Have you ever experienced a pure state of mindfulness?

Have you ever been so involved in the moment that you lost track of time?

Achieving happiness through flow occurs when you place your trust in the guidance of your spirit.

Why is flow important to you?

What is holding you back from experiencing the full depths of life?

Are you concerned about what others will think, feel, or say about your personal transformation?

ACHIEVING THE STATE OF FLOW

1.) Place yourself in a meditative state, focusing your mind, body, and spirit. Be certain that all worldly distractions are set aside.

2.) Define your goals, your ambitions, and your desires when entering this state of meditation.

3.) Challenge the negative by focusing on the positive of life.

4.) Make a plan. If you want to overcome a negative habit, define it, acknowledge it, accept it, claim responsibility for it, and diligently pursue it.

5.) Be engaged; attract that which you desire. When you are intentionally engaged, you are in the present moment.

6.) Be attentive, paying close attention to your internal and external needs.

7.) Be motivated. No one else can achieve or receive the merits of happiness on your behalf.

8.) Be clear with your desires. Don't think that life will simply provide your desires if you patiently wait for them. You must ask; then shall you receive.

9.) Be you. It is important that you allow your spiritual being to shine through each request and moment of this exercise.

Relax and Meditate Daily	Journal Your Inner Thoughts	Practice Focused Breathing

CHAPTER TWENTY

THE PATH TO HAPPINESS

Most people would rather be certain they're miserable than risk being happy.

—Robert Anthony

Many years ago, I had an opportunity to read the poem by Robert Frost, "The Road Not Taken." Robert Frost illustrates, how we are often faced with a dichotomy of choices. Whether we choose the path of lest resistance or the path uncommonly traveled, can determine our life experiences and pursuits.

Two roads diverged in a wood, and I—
I took the one less traveled by,
And that has made all the difference.
—Robert Frost

The path on our journey to happiness will not be a path heavily traveled. Why, you ask? Because a majority of humankind will seek out paths commonly traveled. Those who desire real happiness understand that it is a sacrificial process that develops our internal being. As we develop, we will learn that there are no reasons or rationales for being offended, reactive, vulnerable, obsessive, ashamed, or to blame others. Real peace will alleviate all stress and anxiety, placing fear long behind you. Real peace can be experienced on a continuum, but it takes perseverance, dedication, and motivation to achieve such stillness of our hearts, minds, and spirits. Real peace and happiness understand that you have made mistakes, that we have all made mistakes, but sees our mistakes as mere challenges in the process of life. It is the sort of peace that passeth all understanding and comprehension. As humans, we are all mini-scientists, philosophers, and thinkers, but a problem occurs when we allow the human intellect to believe that we can comprehend and rationally understand all aspects of life. The danger lies in the human mind, because we choose to frequently challenge the spiritual, thus relying on the fallible aspects of our physical mind. If you really desire to change the pathways of your mind, you must

126

lay aside all preconceived notions of life. You must allow the spiritual mind to have a place in your life, therefore following its pathways down the road of life.

> Where you end up isn't the most important thing. It's the road you take to get there. The road you take is what you'll look back on and call your life.

> —Tim Wiley

Have you ever taken a vacation? If so, then you know what it is like to prepare for a vacation. You understand the mindset, the personal exertion, and the mental and physical effort needed to prepare for such an event. The preparation for beginning a vacation is liberating, exhilarating, and typically a direct example of mindfulness. You are rarely closer to mindfulness than when you are leaving all of your normal routines of life behind you. It can be literally a thrill a minute as you prepare for this momentous occasion to rid yourself of life's daily worries. Why, then, do you only choose to live life when you are preparing for a vacation? Or is it the vacation mindset?

Life is a purposeful action. When I choose to live life, I am choosing to be in the present moment. I am choosing to be in a present state. I am choosing to be completely mindful and in harmony with my spiritual nature.

Living life means that you must place all of your worldly concerns, fears, anxieties, and troubles in the hands of your spirit. You must delight in the unification of your spirit with the highest spirit. You are committing yourself to fully living life abundantly, naturally, and unconditionally. In the spiritual realm, there are no fears to be had and no pasts to reflect on. You are neither your successes nor your failures. You are spirit, and the capacity is within you to live life abundantly, freely and completely. Living life begins today, and it can begin within you.

As you begin the process of mastering your life, understand that this process will never be complete until the day that your life unites with the spiritual world. Therefore, the process you have begun should become a lifelong pursuit. It is not unlike physical fitness; with each day of activity, exercise, and healthy habits, your life will transform into a life unlike you could have ever imagined. Your life will become a life that you always dreamt of, a life full of abundance, peace, and complete satisfaction.

CHAPTER CHALLENGE: THE ROAD OF LIFE

REDESIGNING OUR CORE BELIEFS

> In spite of everything, I still believe that people are really good at heart. I simply can't build up my hopes on a foundation consisting of confusion, misery, and death.
>
> —Anne Frank

Your core beliefs are the central part of your internal belief system. Your belief system, at its core, is no different than your physical core. Your physical core is made up of the muscles around your abdominal cavity and your lower back. Reflective of your physical core, your belief system is made up of the vital thoughts and beliefs that you have formed about yourself. Redesigning your belief system occurs when you identify its foundations. The foundation of your personal belief system is made of thoughts, perceptions, life experiences, interactions, and relationships. Your belief system is located in your subconscious and conscious minds. It is the core of who you are, or at least who you think yourself to be. The reality is that our foundations are often mismanaged, misguided, and misdirected. Redesigning your belief system will occur when you begin to identify the basic makeup of that belief system.

What are some of your basic beliefs?

How would you define them?

What are the core beliefs that you hold about yourself? Your spirit? Others? Life?

Are you capable of determining the origins of your beliefs?

What are the foundations of your belief system?

Do you still rely on the foundations of your childhood?

Have you gained or redefined your belief systems as an adult? What are they? How do they guide you as a person and as a spirit?

STRENGTHENING OUR CORE BELIEFS

> Believe you can, believe you can't. Either way, you are correct.
>
> —Henry Ford

Your conscious and your subconscious will accept whatever you place into them. They are only capable of accepting information; they are not decision makers of what is gathered. Therefore, it is critically important that you monitor what messages are derived from the conscious and unconscious states. It is important that you, as a spiritual being, recognize that there are a variety of messages that may develop within your conscious and unconscious minds, but it is your responsibility to define, shape, structure, and filter the information within these messages.

Through the action of thinking about your core beliefs, you have already begun the process of changing these beliefs. Not all of our beliefs are false, so it is important to distinguish between the beliefs that are false and the ones that are true in nature. False beliefs tend to focus us on our inabilities, our failures, our limitations, our weaknesses, and—ultimately—our past. Our true beliefs have the opposite message; they see us as unconditional. Our spirit yearns for these types of messages to be played. Our spirit wants to be recognized as good, valuable, and cherished. It is our spirit that guides us to the truth, liberating us from the bondage of the past and our perceived failures. It is our spirit that makes us better people on this planet.

How would you define your core beliefs?

Create a list of your positive core beliefs. Do you believe them? Why?

Are there core beliefs that you would like to adapt or redefine?

Relax and Meditate Daily	Journal Your Inner Thoughts	Practice Focused Breathing

TRANSFORMING OUR CORE BELIEFS

> The thing always happens that you really believe in, and
> the belief in a thing makes it happen.
>
> —Frank Lloyd Wright

We are capable of changing our belief system. Along this journey of
your discourse of change, you will find that change is rather simple and
progressive. Do not be discouraged if you have fallbacks, but transform
those fallbacks into a progressive movement forward. Follow-through may
be difficult. Do not give up. You will succeed. It is the belief that you will
succeed that will carry you through the challenging times. Ultimately, it
is your choice to transform your belief system.

In the following task, you are to define your current positive beliefs and
the beliefs that you aspire to obtain.

Current beliefs	Aspiring beliefs
I create my own destiny.	I am unconditionally accepting of myself.
I am empathetic.	I unconditional love myself.
I am positively influential.	I am a champion of living life.

Relax and Meditate Daily	Journal Your Inner Thoughts	Practice Focused Breathing

CHAPTER TWENTY-ONE

LIVING

Every man dies. Not every man really lives.

—William Ross Wallace

Living. For years, I waited to live. For many years, I shielded myself from the truth of happiness and pretended that happiness was some sort of outwardly expressive symbol. I avoided searching for happiness, for I had been told what happiness was through various media. Through my friends, my family, and—surprisingly—even my enemies, I had been informed of the meaning of happiness. A host of life's interactions informed me of what real happiness was, but it almost always alluded to an outward expression rather than an inner tranquility. In fact, for many years I carried the following words around in my body, my mind, and my spirit:

> My soul yearns for forgiveness, truth, and liberation of my spirit;
> My heart yields for tomorrow, for today I have made plenty of mistakes; and
> My body waits to live, like a plane on a tarmac full of passengers all seeking to move forward.

My life was not a symbol of living. I had avoided living life in a genuine and wholehearted way. Although I may have lived at my conception, my life had become enamored with life's trials, tribulations, and turmoils. I had lost all perspective of what life is or was for many, many years. I had lost my desire for living. I had not lived in a long, long time. You may be saying to yourself, "How do you know that you are living today?" Here is an answer from a man who had been broken, twisted, and renewed as a human and a spiritual being. For years, I carried the burdens of my past, whether they were my own personal errors or unfortunately embarked upon, when boarding the life of someone else. I had carried many burdens in my life. I ask that you take a moment to imagine what life would be like if, and only if, you were capable of living outside of your burdens, outside of your past. Think of what life would be like if the burdens that you may have caused and the burdens others have placed on you were eliminated from you mind, body, and spirit. Take a moment and think of what would life look like without these heavy-ladened burdens.

On my journey of life, I have discovered many paths that have renewed my perspective of life. During my voyage, I have experienced a happiness that can be lived on a continuum. Let me refresh your mind about the truth of happiness. Happiness is not an elated display or expression; rather, it is a peace that goes beyond all explanations. It is a peace that transcends all of our mistakes, errors, misjudgments, and mishaps in life. It is the sort of peace that allows the broken to feel mended. It is the sort of peace that takes no thought of tomorrow but rather seeks to pursue a life lived in the moment. It is the sort of peace that unites your mind, body, and spirit, allowing them to live in a world of authentic harmony. Have you ever had a moment in which your mind experienced peace? Have you ever had something that burdened your heart? Have you ever had one message in your head conflicting with another message deep inside your soul? If so, you get it—your mind, your body, and your spirit are separate entities residing in one capsule of life. We are a being created with a mind, a body, and a spirit. Living life begins within you.

Are you ready to live life? Or are you going to continue making excuses? Are you going to wait for another day to experience life on a continuum? It is possible to live life on a continuum. It is possible to live life abundantly and full of internal richness. You may be asking yourself, "How can I live life if I am shackled to my problems?" You can't! You must forgive yourself of all errors that you made in life. "What if I have wronged someone else?" you ask. First and foremost, you must forgive yourself. Secondly, follow your spirit. In some cases, you must ask others to forgive you, too. It is sort of ironic, but we tend to hang onto to our pasts much longer than those whom we have perceivably harmed do. Therefore, you may find that if you have wronged another, they may have already forgiven you. Forgiveness is not a denial of our wrongs, but rather a peace when we accept personal responsibility for the wrongs that we have committed. It is also accepting that we do not have to be defined by the wrongs that we have committed.

You may be thinking to yourself, "But I have lost loved ones whom I felt harmed." How do you want those of importance in your life to live life beyond you? Do you want them to live in the past, or do you want them to pursue the abundance of life? Personally, when my life expires, I want my friends and family to continue to diligently pursue life. I want them to experience life beyond all explanations, and I want them to life abundantly. If I choose to avoid life, then those around me may also choose to emulate my own life, therefore choosing to avoid life altogether. What do you want for those whom know you best?

Living life is something that has been discussed since the spark of human thought. We have philosophized and theorized the meaning of life until we are blue in the face. We have speculated the beyond and debated our future. When was the last time you made a conscious effort to live life in the moment? Are you consciously and spiritually living in harmony?

Living life is a daily effort. If you wait to live, life will never become the reality that you want it to be.

CHAPTER CHALLENGE: LIVING LIFE BEYOND

> It is only possible to live happily ever after on a day-to-day basis.
>
> —Margaret Bonnano

Living life—what's holding you back? What are you clinging to that continuously returns you to your past? Are you ready to move your life forward? Are you excited about the opportunity to be reborn as a person and a spirit? Life can be experienced daily. Life can be lived abundantly. You, too, can renew the spiritual being that resides within you. You, too, can experience life at its fullest. Let's begin living today. Let's start looking at each day as an opportunity to live life.

We are not intended to live life in the past. We are intended to live life now. When we were children, we were not concerned with our histories, because we had no histories to cling to. We were not concerned about the future, because we knew that our future would arrive soon enough. We were concentrated on living each moment. We were alive and fully present in every aspect of our lives. Our greatest concern was the now, the present moment. We were always seeking new ways to enjoy life, to explore life, to find a way to play each day. As we matured physically, we began to dismiss the right to live. We sought out excuses why we could not live. We placed our minds on what happened in the past, placing aspirations on what may occur in the future. We became resentful of the now and the present. We were no longer living.

So, how can I return myself to a state of living life and living it abundantly? Living life begins the moment that you request it. It begins the moment that it becomes a need. Our spiritual being needs daily nutrition, daily recognition, daily communication. When we begin to experience this sort of life again, we will notice a drastic change in all aspects of life. Our five senses will be enriched. The pleasures of this life will be richly increased and appreciated. Our being will be transformed from a state of waiting to live to an excitement of how we will live the next moment in our lives. It will be as though you were awakened from a long slumber, having slept for generations. You will have no regrets of the past, and no desire to anticipate the future. You will be ready to live life today, living it abundantly.

Now let's begin living life, living it abundantly.

The following exercises will increase your life:

Meditative Wandering

As you set out for a walk, intend on spending time with your mind, body, and spirit. As you begin this exercise, you will find that it is difficult at times, but—not unlike other forms of exercising—it will eventually become a regular routine to improving your life. Focus your mind, body, and spirit on the positive flow of life with the intention of increasing your life. Follow the flow, enjoying this pleasurable experience. Focus your mind, body, and spirit on how they, too, will continue to grow, explore, and have opportunities to set out on new adventures. The primary point of this exercise is to shift your mind, body, and spirit to the positive.

Meditative Watching

As you set out on this meditative experience, find a place of peacefulness, joyfulness, and harmony. Consider taking yourself to a park, a wilderness, or a national forest. Spend time thinking on the positive. Place your mind on the beauty of your environment. Enjoy the gentle falling of the leaves, the whisper of the wind, and the splashing of the water against the banks of the shore. The primary point of this exercise is to unite your spiritual being with the spiritual aspects of nature.

Free-Flow Journaling

The free-flow journaling exercise is intended to connect your spiritual being with the spiritual world. It is intended to unite your spirit with your mind and body. The free-flow journaling exercise occurs when you focus your mind on nothing, simply letting your spirit guide you. Allow your spirit to guide you and write whatever enters your mind. Try this exercise; it is an awesome experience.

Love Letters

Write a love letter to yourself, your friends, your family, or anyone who have a significant place in your heart, mind, and spirit. Write a letter expressing the positive qualities of this person. Let the letter form itself. Let your spirit guide you while you transpose this letter. Such inspirational messages can prove profitable and meaningful to those who receive them.

Let your love letter be a beacon of hope, love, joy, and happiness. Try writing yourself such letters on a frequent basis.

Conscious and Subconscious Relaxation

Conscious and subconscious relaxation is a journey of unification of your mind, body, and spirit. It will take time for you to formalize a rhythmic understanding of how to relax the trinity of you, but in time you will become unified within your being. It is the purposeful concentration on relaxing. Be certain when pursuing such a meditative state that your environment is conducive to it. Be clear with your intentions, not allowing your mind to clutter your thoughts with negative pathways. In your state of relaxation, you will need to find a place of peacefulness and harmony. A soft couch, bed, or comfortable mat might be an ideal setting. As you journey down this path towards relaxation, be certain that you have a goal in mind. Focus your attention on your goal, allowing the flow of life to guide you through this process. You might want to develop a mental scene of serenity, calmness, and unity. It may be important to think of this as your personal oasis. Enjoy the moment. Savor the moment. Allow yourself to meditate on the positives of life and the spiritual world. Do not forget to breathe throughout this exercise. It will be a time of total relaxation and spiritual guidance. May the peace, joy, and abundance of life bless you during this experience.

Expanding Your Vocabulary

Communication is the embodiment of the words we choose to use. Words act as fuel, empowering our ability to communicate. By expanding your vocabulary, you mobilize words to speak for you. You increase your ability to communicate your needs, wants, and desires. Through the improvement of your vocabulary, you are capable of becoming a virtual lexicon that can act as a defense against the spirit of negativity and a bridge to positivity. Broadening your ability to communicate, you have intentionally opened pathways that might have otherwise been closed to you. When we are capable of connecting words to our emotions and our feelings, we have more insight into our human and spiritual conditions. It is through the learning of words that you develop your cognitive and spiritual minds.

Relax and Meditate Daily	Journal Your Inner Thoughts	Practice Focused Breathing

LIVING CHALLENGES: CONTINUED WORK
                                    BEYOND THIS BOOK

Peace is not something you wish for; it's something
you make, something you do, something you are, and
something you give away.

—Robert Fulghum

The following exercises have been developed to help you continue your
tour of your mind, body, and spirit. These living challenges are simply
instruments devised to help you continue your progress towards a healthier
you. These challenges are merely examples of avenues that you can pursue.
It is important that you recognize that you have the instruments inside of
you. You have your own set of living challenges, but it is not uncommon
that those challenges have been silenced. Through the practice of these
living challenges, you will become aware of your own personal living
challenges residing in you.

May the following living challenges prove beneficial to your mind, body
and spirit.

May your life become a blessing to others.

May your mind, body, and spirit guide you through the remainder of your
life.

May the peace of the spirit reside within you, and may you never wait to
live again.

JOURNALING: EXPRESSING YOUR
                                    INNERMOST THOUGHTS

Journaling is an incredible exercise that stimulates your mind, your body, and your spirit. It is an exercise that can unite your spirit with the spiritual world. It is an excellent source for expressing yourself, clarifying your ambitions, and solving difficult problems. Journaling uses both hemispheres of the brain, which ultimately means that you are exercising your complete physical mind. The exercise of journaling can help with fears, temptations, uncertainties, and confusion. Furthermore, journaling is beneficial for increasing one's awareness, self-esteem, self-worth, and personal insights. Finally, journaling is the most beneficial when you are willing to be authentically you.

Today's date: _____

Journal title: _____

DEFINING LOVE

What is your definition of love?

Do you see yourself as a loving person?

Do you love yourself as you love others?

What does it mean to live an unconditional life?

Our definition of love is frequently a makeup of our families influence, our relationship encounters, and our personal insights into self. Have you equated love with peace? Do you feel that love and peace are interactive and interrelated? Defining love is different than living a life abundant of love. Love is an unconditional state of being. Love is a merciful, gentle, and passionate embodiment of the spirit that resides in us. If you unconditionally love someone, you look beyond their inadequacies, fleshly errors, and simple mistakes, seeing them as a being full of life and potential. Love goes beyond the superficial, hearkening deep inside the human spirit. Love calls for patience, kindness, peacefulness, and sincerity. Love is abundant, and it is free. Love looks beyond our faults, our failures, and our mistakes.

Did you know that many religions and faiths teach that love always hopes, protects, preserves, and trusts?

Genuine love, authentic love, and unconditional love are characteristics of our spirit.

Can you imagine life without an unconditional form of love? What if all loves were represented by the commonly misspoken, misinterpreted, miscommunicated, and misguided forms of love? What am I speaking of? Have you ever heard someone declare, "Man, I love my car" or "I love my new outfit/relationship/house" or some other earthly possession? If so, then you have heard someone misuse, miscommunicate, and misinterpret the real meaning of love. Love knows no boundaries. It contains no envy or self-righteousness. Real love, genuine love, and authentic love can only be known through the leadership of spirit.

Try this as an exercise: Journal the names of those you undoubtedly love. Then look at those names and ask yourself, "Do I unconditionally love them? What if they failed me?" Then write your own name. Ask yourself if there is any form of failure that would cause you to stop loving yourself. If there is, then you have placed conditions on those particular relationships. If there isn't, then you are well on your way to living life and living it abundantly.

LIFE QUESTIONNAIRE

The following questionnaire asks about feelings that you may have throughout your life. Please answer the questions truthfully and forthrightly. Please mark the appropriate answer. Please remember that each of these questions is central to helping you improve your overall quality of life.

1.) During my life, I have made many mistakes.
   □ True   □ False

2.) I feel that I am responsible for others' happiness and well-being.
   □ True   □ False

3.) I seldom feel comfortable in my own skin.
   □ True   □ False

4.) I desire to please and be reassured by others.
   □ True   □ False

5.) I frequently reflect on my past.
   □ True   □ False

6.) My mistakes cause me great pain.
   □ True   □ False

7.) I often feel awkward and inadequate in social gatherings.
   □ True   □ False

8.) I do not feel comfortable with the opposite sex.
   □ True   □ False

9.) I blame myself for my mistakes.
   □ True   □ False

10.) I am not comfortable reflecting on my past.
   □ True   □ False

11.) I am an overly sensitive person.
   □ True   □ False

12.) I have a hard time loving others.
☐ True   ☐ False

13.) I feel uncomfortable being around positive people.
☐ True   ☐ False

14.) I have a difficult time receiving love.
☐ True   ☐ False

15.) I can't forgive myself for my past mistakes.
☐ True   ☐ False

There are no right or wrong answers here, but it is important for you to recognize how you responded to these questions. If you have primarily marked *True* as an answer, then it is important that you recognize the importance of forgiveness, love, and personal acceptance. If you have primarily answered *False* to these questions, then you are well on your way to encountering a truly peace-centered life.

Being aware of our emotional baggage is half the battle. Do not be dismayed if you have primarily marked *True*, but be encouraged that you will one day overcome your negative state. Take heed of your answers and realize that you are a person deserving of an unconditional life.

CHANGING YOUR DIET

Did you know that your diet can affect your overall psychological health? There is a direct correlation between diet and your overall physical and psychological health. You may want to consider detoxifying your body through diet and lifestyle changes. A majority of research suggests that you should have an intake of 50–60% alkaline-forming foods and 30–40% acid-forming foods. Consult your physician or a nutritionist if you are seeking to restore your health through diet or diet substitution.

The following are a few suggestions that may prove beneficial for your physical health:

1.) The reduction or elimination of consumption of caffeine and sugar
2.) An increase in consumption of purified or filtered water, fruit juices, and vegetable drinks
3.) The reduction or elimination of consumption of animal proteins
4.) An increase in consumption of fresh vegetables and fruit
5.) The reduction or elimination of consumption of nicotine, alcohol, and illegal drugs
6.) The reduction or elimination of consumption of foods that produce acid- or alkaline-forming toxins. (It is important that any changes to your diet are regulated by a dietician, nutritionist, or physician.)
7.) An increase in consumption of fiber.
8.) An addition of supplements to your diet. (It is important to discuss such changes with a pharmacist or physician.)
9.) A regular routine of exercise. This is highly recommended for your mind, body, and spirit.

If you have questions or concerns about your overall dietary consumption, you should consult with a health professional. It is important to understand that dietary changes can have a profound effect on your overall health. Be certain to consult with your physician or a nutritionist before making drastic changes to your diet.

ENHANCING YOUR LIFE

You should strive to spend 30 to 40 minutes thinking and reading on spiritual topics.

You should be certain that you exercise daily. The newest research shows that we should exercise anywhere between 30 minutes to 1 1/2 hours a day.

You should intend on being in the company of friends, family, and others that lift your spirit.

You should be certain to have natural laughter as a part of your daily routine. If you have trouble laughing, try laughing aloud in the mirror. It may take sometime for it to become natural, but in time you should begin having daily laughter as a part of your life.

You should spend at least 30 to 40 minutes daily reading positive literature. Positive literature will remind you of areas that need improvement, strengthen areas that are in need, and confirm areas in which you have solid strength. Remember, there is never anything wrong with having limitations or challenges. Be aware of your limitations and face your challenges head on.

DESIGNING OUR OWN LIVING CHALLENGES

> At the center of your being you have the answer; you know
> who you are and you know what you want.
>
> —Lao Tzu

Design your own living challenge. Let your spirit be your guide. Living challenges do not have meaning for others; rather, they must meet a need within you. You are the guide of your living challenges.

Following are life challenges to consider:

1.) Be inventive.
2.) Be constructive.
3.) Fix something.
4.) Complete a task.
5.) Exercise your mind, body, and spirit.
6.) Resolve past conflicts.
7.) Look to your natural world for remedies.
8.) Create solutions for your problems.
9.) Consider designing your own self-help exercise.
10.) Be proactive.
11.) Redesign tools for your own personal use.
12.) Keep your mind on spiritually relevant topics.
13.) Be artistic.
14.) Meditate on your design, asking for inspiration from your spiritual being.

ACKNOWLEDGEMENTS

COVER DESIGN

Jason Hirsch, *Graphic Designer*

Jason Hirsch has collaborated with Dr. Asa Don Brown on the concept of the cover of this book. Jason Hirsch graduated in 1997 from the Art Institute of Colorado with a degree in Visual Communications. He has since worked as a Broadcast Designer and Motion Graphics Artist for on-air television news since completing his education. He has produced graphics for the American Networks, NBC, ABC, and CBS. Mr. Hirsch has had a bright career working in various mediums of art and graphic design including print, web, video and a variety of on-air forums. Mr. Hirsch has received a multiple number of recognitions and awards including:

6 Emmy Awards and 3 Colorado Broadcaster Awards.

I am personally grateful for Jason Hirsch's dedication, artistic comprehension, and willingness to create a truly magnificent cover for this book. If you are seeking a graphic designer for your business or artistic concepts you should contact Jason Hirsch. I unequivocally recommend Jason Hirsch as a Graphic Designer and as a person.

You can reach Jason Hirsch through his website at:
jasonhirschdesign.com

ARTISTIC AND PHOTOGRAPHIC WORKS

Photographs and Artistic concepts were created with the help of:

Dr. Tracy Lynn Brown (Optometrist, British Columbia), Leah May Brown (L. B. Creations, Texas), and Dr. Asa Don Brown. I am sincerely grateful for the time dispensed to develop the artwork within this book. I feel that the photographs and artwork enrich the overall content of the book.

CONTACTING DR. ASA DON BROWN

Please feel free to contact the offices of Dr. Asa Don Brown. You can obtain more information on Dr. Brown and his on workshops, seminars, books, audio and video merchandise through his website (www.asadonbrown. com). Dr. Brown looks forward to having an opportunity to work with you.